BIBLICAL
MANHOOD

Masculinity, Leadership and Decision Making

Stuart Scott

DEDICATION

Dedicated to
My son, Marc Scott
My son-in-law, Travis Goldstein
and
My grandson, River Ray Goldstein

CONTENTS

APPENDICES

Chapter One
FIRST THINGS FIRST
God's Provisions for Man

If you have opened this book and you are a man, you may have done so thinking, "Now here's a book a man can use!" or "Ah yes, the three things that often get me into trouble!" And trouble, indeed, is what we have if we are not *God's* kind of "real man." Being such a man certainly involves a holy perspective of the three qualities that are in the title of this book. However, one thing is for sure: We can never possess the understanding or the power to pull these off as our creator intended without taking hold of his most basic provisions for our *greatest* needs as a man. We must first be in a right and real relationship with God and thereby be given a new kind of heart. We must recognize our need for God himself, forgiveness and His power in our lives.

God has graciously and specifically provided for our needs as a man. He has made a way for our salvation, our sanctification, and our glorification. If you partake of these three provisions you can become the man you were created to be.

1.   God's provision of salvation

God has provided a Savior in the person of Jesus Christ. Amazingly, He was willing to pay the penalty for the sin that *we* owe. This means that even though Jesus lived a sinless life, He, Almighty God, left heaven and the adoration He deserves in order to endure the conditions of this world, suffer shame, be rejected by men, die a criminal's gruesome death, bear the guilt of all our sins, be bitterly rejected by the Father (with whom He knew only love and harmony), and suffer the hell we so richly deserve (Philippians 2:6-8). Only Christ could do what was necessary to bring us to God.

> **For Christ also died for sins once for all, the just for the unjust, so that He might** *bring us to God*, **having been put to death in the flesh, but made alive in the spirit.**
> **1 Peter 3:18 [emphasis mine]**

It was through Christ's suffering and rejection on the cross that God's righteous wrath against sin was satisfied and a way to obtain forgiveness was made (Romans 5:9). This forgiveness is possible because God is willing to exchange Christ's righteousness for our sinfulness (2 Corinthians 5:21). For this exchange to take place a husband must have saving faith. Saving faith involves:

- Acknowledging the true reason for our existence and God's full right to our lives and how we live them (Matthew 16:24-26; Romans 11:36; 1 Corinthians 6:20).
- Coming to God in humbleness, recognizing you have nothing to offer God in your defense (James 4:6).
- Asking Him for His mercy and forgiveness, instead of what is deserved (Luke 18:9-14).
- Believing in who Christ is and His payment for your sin (1 Corinthians 15:3).
- Believing that Christ rose from the dead as Lord over all and sits at the right hand of the Father pleading the case of all those who believe (1 Corinthians 15:4; Philippians 2:9-11; Hebrews 7:25).

Christ also taught that in order to enter the kingdom of God we must be like a little child. This may smack at our manly pride but Christ was talking about important attitudes of the heart. A little child knows his place and has humble faith. A little child is dependent and needy. We must come to God with this kind of faith in order to receive His gift of salvation.

> **"Truly I say to you, whoever does not receive the kingdom of God like a child will by no means enter it at all."**
> **Mark 10:15**

If we really contemplate saving faith, we can understand why Christ said what He did to those who came to hear Him speak.

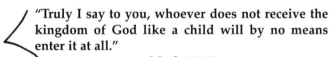

> **"Enter through the narrow gate; for the gate is wide and the way is broad that leads to destruction, and there are many who enter through it. For the gate is small and the way is narrow that leads to life, and** *there are few who find it.***"**
> **Matthew 7:13-14 [emphasis mine]**

Don't be deceived. A prayer said or a profession made in the past should not assure you of your salvation. Are you *having* saving faith *now*? Are you believing *now*? It is an ongoing (obedient and persevering) belief that demonstrates that you are a child of God. Christ offered this warning to all who would listen,

> "Not everyone who says to Me, 'Lord, Lord,' will enter the kingdom of heaven."
> **Matthew 7:21a**

If you have never yielded to God's plan (to be forgiven and walk with Him) I beseech you, take time right now to talk to Him about these things. Ask Him to be merciful to you, not because you deserve it, but because you know that He is the Lord God who created the universe. Confess your sins (of motive, thought, word and deed) to God and seek His forgiveness on the basis of Christ's payment for your sin. If you come to God in humility and with saving faith, He will grant you salvation.

> [Jesus said] "All that the Father gives Me will come to Me, and the one who comes to Me I will certainly not cast out."
> **John 6:37**

2. God's provision of sanctification   *progressive*

Salvation does not automatically cause us to be all that we should be. Not by a long shot! It does, however, mean that we will wholeheartedly enter into a dependent effort with God toward *change* into Christlikeness (Philippians 3:12-14; 2 Peter 3:18). We do this moment by moment because of and by the Power of the gospel. In our daily lives we must remember and apply the gospel truths. (Christ's life, Christ's death for our sin, Christ in us, Christ for us, etc.)

Sometimes we may be inclined to believe that little can be done to change our ways, but obviously this is wrong. Once we are saved, God initiates the sanctification or *growth process*. God Himself provides His Word, His Spirit, prayer, and His Church for our growth (2 Peter 1:2-11). Without these provisions we could not change in the least. On the other hand, God commands that we "exercise ourselves unto godliness" (1Timothy 4:7-9). What does this mean? The Greek word for "exercise" (*gumnazo*) is where our words gymnasium and gymnastics come from. This means that with prayer for God's help we are to put a strenuous effort into becoming more like Christ. When we do our part, we must also trust in God's work and God's promise, on the basis of what Christ did on the cross for us.

Hope

> **For I am confident of this very thing, that He who began a good work in you will perfect it until the day of Christ Jesus.**
> **Philippians 1:6**

When we do our part as a Christian, we are cooperating with God in the growth process. We do our part, first of all, by *devoting our lives to loving and living for Him, rather than self*. When a person truly comes to faith in Christ he will have a new passion—Christ.

> **And He died for all, so that they who live should no longer live for themselves, but for Him who died and rose again on their behalf.**
> **2 Corinthians 5:15**

We are to be so devoted to our Creator, that we labor to please Him with every fiber of our being. Our love for the God who created and saved us should be so great that walking with Him is more important to us than anything else in the world.

Dependently working with God in the change process also means that *we will deal with any known sin God's way*. Some people believe that God's way of dealing with sin is to simply confess it and ask forgiveness. The Bible teaches that we are to deal with our sin in a fuller and much more practical way.

When we sin, God wants us to do three things: *SIN*

- Confess to God our sin and our resolve to change toward righteousness. (Proverbs 28:13; 1 John 1:9)
- Rejoice in forgiveness through Christ (Matthew 6:12).
- Ask God for His transforming grace to change. (Psalm 25:4; John 15:5).
- Repent according to God's process for change by:

4

a. *Working to renew the mind with Scripture* . (Romans 12:1-2). This involves knowing Scripture about whatever sin issue is at hand well enough to *specifically* change wrong or incomplete thinking into thinking that is in agreement with God's principles and promises. We must purposefully guard and renew our minds.

Replacing Sinful Thoughts

Sinful Thoughts, Void of God	Thankful, Trusting, Hopeful Thoughts
I've had it! I can't take this job anymore. (discouragement / giving up)	Lord, You know all about this difficult situation. Thank you that I have a job and that you can help me to endure. I pray that you might supply a different job if that is best. (Philippians 2:14; 4:13)
I just want to be left alone. (selfishness) - Go away? - Run/Flight	Lord, You know I don't feel like giving right now but I thank you that I have a family and that you can give me your strength. Help me to serve you and others now. (Philippians 2:3-4)
What if I lose my job? (worry)	Lord, I pray that I don't lose my job but if I do, I know that you will somehow provide. I thank you that you are faithful and in control. I trust you. (Matthew 6:25-34)

b. *Working to put off sinful actions and to put on righteous ones* (Ephesians 4:20-24). This involves putting enough thought into one's life to: (1) specifically plan how and when a particular sin will be avoided, and (2) determine specific ways to apply its righteous alternatives. True repentance does not take place without these things.

5

We must renew our minds as we work with God to renew our actions, because our actions flow out of our motives, thoughts and beliefs. This fact can be pictured something like this.

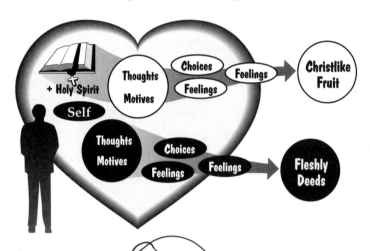

3. God's provision of glorification

God promises to bring us to heaven where He is and to free us from our sinful bent (1 Corinthians 15:50-58). What a great hope we have! This life is not all there is! Our short time on Earth is not what life is even about. Everything is working toward the great end of God's people being with Him for eternity (Revelation 21:3, 7).

AGE?   *CITIZENS OF HEAVEN*

Every Christian needs to be heavenly-minded (Colossians 3:1-3; Matthew 6:33). We will look forward to heaven more if we fully accept the fact that this life is *not* heaven, and never will be. If we live with heaven in our sights we will please God and be less likely to grow weary in the hardships of life (Hebrews 11:8-10; 12:1-3). Remembering that we will see Jesus face to face one day can also have a very purifying affect on our lives (1 John 3:2-3). We should strive to keep an eternal perspective and place *all* our hope in our future with Christ.

> Therefore, prepare your minds for action, keep sober in spirit, fix your hope completely on the grace to be brought to you at the revelation of Jesus Christ.
>
> **1 Peter 1:13**

Chapter Two
PROFILING CHRISTIAN MASCULINITY

There are many ways to characterize a "real man" in our culture today. It certainly involves more than refusing to eat *quiche*! If we are to have a biblical worldview we must definitely look at our view of what a man is. Basic beliefs about our sex, who we are and what we should be like greatly impacts our own gender evaluations as well as the shaping of boys, the education of young men, the success of marriage, the effectiveness of the Church in the world, and even the stability of society. Further, our view of manhood affects our attitudes, our character, and our interaction with one another.

In some very key ways, men and women *are* the same but they were not created to be exactly the same: "male and female he created them" (Genesis 1:27). There are not only opposing opinions over whether there is any significant difference between the sexes, but also over what those differences really are. Christians need a clear understanding of what distinguishes a man from a woman, *according to their Creator.* This chapter will be devoted to understanding what *true masculinity* is and is not. The question, "How does a man know if he is a *real man?*" will be discovered from Scripture. In doing so, we will discover both the basis and the catalyst for developing better leadership qualities and skills. A real man *will* lead, and *will* strive to be the *right kind* of leader.

Imagine this topic being discussed on one of America's college campuses today. The ideas expressed would be as varied as the many strong opinions found there. One might hear,

- "A man should be macho and self-reliant."
- "A man should be interdependent and sensitive."
- "A real man must be romantic."
- "All boys should be raised to be good at sports in order to express their masculinity and relate to other men."
- "A man's man is successful and a leader."
- "A respected man sees himself as an equal; a non-leader, as a fifty-fifty partner."

- "A man is not a man unless he can rule his family without any questioning from them."

How can there be so many opinions among supposedly learned individuals? There are at least two key reasons: the sinfulness of man and the loss of absolutes.

Sinfulness Affects One's Concept of Masculinity

The history of the world's concept of masculinity is a sad commentary on how far man has strayed from God's original intent. It is a confusing and disappointing history. In the beginning, of course, God created the perfect man—Adam. He, being created by the perfect Creator, was the epitome of true masculinity. However, shortly after Adam's creation, his soul and body were gravely affected by his choice to sin (the Fall: Genesis 3:1-8). From that point on, left to himself, man's depravity (inherent sinfulness) pushes him to stray in every aspect of life (Jeremiah 17:9). Masculinity is just one of the areas that have been corrupted. One does not have to look far beyond the Fall to see the effects of depravity on the concept of masculinity.

Depraved ideas about what is *manly* have affected men and women negatively through the ages. In the ancient world, there was everything from the mild mistreatment of women to full-scale barbarism. In the early Greek culture, "real men" looked down on their wives as mere child bearers and housekeepers. They also did not allow them at the dinner table or in any assembly. In the Roman culture, women were no more than a means to legally bear children as well as a temporary fancy that could be discarded on a whim (JoAnn Shelton, *As the Romans Did*. New York: Oxford University Press, 1998, 37-55). In contrast, men living in a matriarchal society were absorbed into their wife's family, followed the mother-in-law's or the grandmother's lead, and faded into the background. Throughout history, some cultures have devised rather extreme ways for young men to prove their masculinity or manhood. While it is not necessarily wrong to have a visible rite of passage ceremony for young men, it has historically been a *very* bad idea for a man to have something to prove! In America, the feminist movement came on the scene at least partially in reaction to actual injustices by men against women. With the passing of time, that movement has grown into a far-reaching, immoral catalyst that has further confused and even redefined the lines of gender.

A Loss of Absolutes Affects One's Concept of Masculinity

In more recent Western history, the increasing relativism (the belief that there is no ultimate standard) and the resulting individualism ("only I know what is right for me") have had a great impact on gender concepts. This "no absolutes" mentality means that each man is left to his own "wisdom" on the subject of masculinity. That wisdom, of course, is totally subjective and may be based on one's own desires, culture, popular figures, and/or educational training in the academic fields of psychology, sociology, or anthropology. There are a number of reasons why this kind of wisdom will get a person nowhere close to God's standard. First of all, man's own ideas and desires are very often selfish and self-serving. Second, culture has historically followed man's depravity. Third, American role models today basically consist of pathetic, immoral sports figures, movie stars, and rock musicians. Finally, the higher educational systems of the day are for the most part based on the study of unsaved people by unsaved people. As a result, there is a great reluctance on the part of typical Americans to make any statement about what is *truly masculine*. In fact, the earlier hypothetical college discussion might well be cut short with the postmodern declaration that each man must determine for himself what masculinity is and live within that paradigm without imposing his belief on others. This statement could very well be followed by the idea that one really should *not* be thinking in terms of masculinity but genderless individualism.

It is clear from both Scripture and history that the unashamed and unchecked expression of depravity is continually on the increase and the recognition of God's truth is on the decline (2 Timothy 3:1-5). J.I. Packer sees society's decline in this way: "The truth is that because we have lost touch with God and his word we have lost the secret both of community (because sin kills neighbor-love) and of our own identity (because at the deepest level we do not know who or what we are, or what we exist for)" (J.I. Packer, *Knowing Man*. (Westchester, IL: Cornerstone Books, 1978) p. 43).

The first step to regaining a true understanding of masculinity is to acknowledge that man's wisdom is misleading. Here is what the Bible says about personal opinion: "There is a way that seems right to a man, but its end is the way to death" (Proverbs 14:12). Men must not follow the way that seems right to them or to society. In reality, following what seems right about masculinity is doing great damage to men's lives. Young men are floundering and grasping at wrong ways to express their manhood. Marriages are also paying the price. Even many Christian women are regularly lamenting that their husbands are either timid or violent. More men seem to be experiencing depression and abandoning their societal responsibilities during their supposed mid-life crises. In the church, there seems to be a growing dearth of exemplary male leadership. Further complicating the problem for God's people is the rise of "Christian" feminism, which clearly departs from Scripture and the Will of God. On a larger scale, society as a whole has experienced a great and unfortunate loss of the significance of gender. So much so, that it is very acceptable in today's culture to even *deny* one's gender and try to switch to the other.

God's Truth Will Lead the Way

Without an absolute standard, the confusion about masculinity can only worsen. There is no hope of improving people's depraved inclinations or making sense of the confusion. The *Webster's New Collegiate Dictionary* definition of *masculine* is certainly an accurate picture of the ambiguity that surrounds this subject in our culture:

> **Masculine (mas-kyoo-lin)** 1 a: male b: having qualities appropriate to or usually associated with a man.

There is no clear understanding of masculinity because our society because has generally forsaken the only dependable absolute there is—God's Word. Humans need to know what God has to say about man and his masculinity. God's truth is timeless and trans-cultural. Furthermore, it is completely sufficient to be the guide for becoming the kind of men God intended (Psalm 119:105; John 17:17; 2 Peter 1:3). One must, in submission and obedience, align his thinking and actions with Scripture in order to understand and live out masculinity for the right reason: God's glory.

Basic Characteristics of Masculinity

A man cannot begin to be the man God intended him to be unless he fully acknowledges who *mankind* is. God had a design in mind when He created human beings, and He created just what He intended. Those who are unwilling to acknowledge God as Creator will never be fully able to understand who they are or what they should be like. But those who believe in a perfect, good, and personal God and who have been given a new heart by the forgiveness of sins through Jesus Christ can learn greatly from some basic things God has to say about people. God's Word describes at least six basic characteristics of humans that have specific implications as they relate to the subject of masculinity.

1. <u>Man was created in God's image</u> (Genesis 1:27). This means that he finds his identity in the person of God. He is rational, creative, and relational. He has an eternal soul that needs to find its meaning and rest in God alone. Being creative and relational is part of being made in the image of God. Unfortunately, many men try to escape these aspects of their manhood, claiming they are feminine qualities. Furthermore, if a man sees himself as a mere animal, he can excuse all sorts of behavior and uncontrolled passions.

2. <u>Man was created a worshiper</u> (John 4:23; Romans 1:21-25). Because man has been given a soul, he is by nature a "religious" being. He *will* worship something. Though he was given a soul for the purpose of worshiping God alone, his depravity pulls him in other directions. Until he bows the knee to Jesus Christ, he might worship himself, another person, money, success and its accompaniments, false gods, or a myriad of other things. This kind of worship is neither manly nor true. Conversely, it *is* manly to seek and passionately love the God of the Bible.

3. <u>Since the Fall, man has been a sinner by nature</u> (Romans 3:12). Man was not initially created this way, but he *was* created with the ability to rationally choose. Soon he embraced this basic characteristic with his choice to sin against the one and only prohibition that God gave him. Therefore, a man must be

11

aware, contrary to what his pride or his society may tell him, that he can be very wrong. At the core of his very being there is an innate wrongness that will be with him until he reaches heaven. This being true, it is certainly *manly* to admit when he is wrong in his thinking or actions, rather than try to hide it or deny it.

4. <u>Man is in need of God's saving grace</u> (John 3:16; Titus 3:4-7). It stands to reason that when God gave Eve to Adam, making it clear that he was to love and lead her, he would also give him a protective inclination, and strong desire for her salvation. Through the ages men have protected and come to the rescue of women, children, societies, and even ideologies. This kind of courage is a manly thing. However, man must also realize that he also needs a savior and protector. Admitting his utter helplessness and need of salvation is a doubly humbling experience for a courageous man. And yet as we explained earlier, any man who hopes to ever be a real man must acknowledge his need to be saved by God. He must be rescued from himself, the evil one (Satan), and the ensuing judgment for his sin by bowing the knee to Jesus Christ as the only Lord and Savior of his life.

<u>Man was not created self-sufficient but needing God and others</u> (John 15:5; Galatians 5:14; Hebrews 4:16). By virtue of being a created being and a fallen individual, it is obvious that man needs God for even more than salvation. He needs God's enduring strength, guidance, and wisdom. It is also obvious that God made him to need others with statements like, "It is not good for man to be alone" and "I will make him a helper meet for him" (Genesis 2:18). John MacArthur writes, "In marriage men cannot be faithful to the Lord unless they are willingly and lovingly dependent on the wife He has given them" (John MacArthur, Jr. *Different By Design*. Wheaton, IL: Victor Books, 1994 p. 44). Over 30 commands in the Bible pertaining to "one another" reinforce this truism.

5. <u>Man was created to be different from woman</u> (Genesis 1:27). The fact that God created man unlike woman in appearance is a clear indication that they are different in other ways. In His wisdom, God has fashioned them uniquely inside and out, perfectly corresponding to how they are to *be* different and

12

"memo?"

function differently. Before more is said about that, note that there was no mistaking God's desire for an outward difference. Adam and Eve's pre-covering existence in the Garden reveals that God obviously intended for men and women to look different to themselves and others. There is subsequent Scripture to clearly support this fact (Deuteronomy 22:5; 1 Corinthians 11:14-15). A timeless principle that can be observed from all of this is that God wants individuals to clearly express their own given sex. Today, there is less difference in how men and women look, and even act, than ever before in America's history. Though culture is pushing for unisex everything, men and women need be careful that they are distinguishably different from the opposite sex in appearance, mannerisms, and cultural concepts of appropriate gender behavior. Some men might require help to recognize and change effeminate habits which they have inadvertently developed.

Because men and women were created with differences does not mean they are different in every way. Both genders are equal personally and spiritually. No one should argue that women should not be treated with equal appreciation and dignity. Nor should their input or opinions be discounted on either societal or familial levels. Furthermore, the sexes are alike in that they are both able to communicate and even able to cling together as one in marriage. But many want to overlook the existence of the comprehensive difference between a man's and woman's being. By the 1960s and 1970s, the feminist movement took a decidedly new path which has led to a current, full-blown assault on any traditional concept of what constitutes a man or woman (Werner Neuer, *Man & Woman*. Wheaton, IL: Crossway Books, 1991, p. 15-16).

Many are not aware (or perhaps want to overlook) that the differences in God's design for the sexes reaches far beyond outward appearance. These dissimilarities are amazingly and beautifully consistent with the roles He has set forth in Scripture. Much more will be said about roles in chapter 3 as it relates to the husband, but for now let us consider that there is scientific evidence and research that reveal the extensive physiological and personal differences between men and women. Such differences include: bone structure and constitution, muscles, skin, sexual organs and function, blood constitution, bodily liquids, hormones, chromosomal cell structure, cognitive function, abilities, outlooks, and relations. Men and women are distinctly different beings. With this great plan of God in mind John Benton writes, "In particular, gender difference is not fortuitous. It is not a product of chance. It is not something unreasonable and unintelligible. It is not something to be regretted, or to fight against. It is to be gratefully accepted as the good gift of a loving God" (John Benton, *Gender Questions*. England: Evangelical Press, 2000 p. 18).

A man cannot ever be a man in the truest sense unless he, in his mind, attests to these basic realities and gives his life over to them and the One who created him. Masculinity then is a matter of the mind. A man can go to the gym to work out and even gain the physique of Charles Atlas but this will not make him any more masculine. It is important to keep in mind A. B. Bruce's statement, "What tells ultimately is, not what is without a man, but what is within." Masculinity then is a matter of the mind <u>or heart</u>.

Characteristics of the Perfect Man–Jesus

Jesus, the God-Man, is portrayed in the Scriptures as the only perfect man (1 Peter 2:21-22). This being so, He is the perfect picture of what one should strive to be as a man. Christ is the pristine example of masculinity in every way (1 John 2:6). Surely no one would say that any quality He possessed was unmanly. The following is a chart of Christ-like character qualities (attitudes and actions) that will help explain authentic manhood more specifically.

Qualities of the Perfect Man		
ATTITUDES	ACTIONS	REFERENCES
Eternal Mindset	Did the will and work of the Father <small>Not working towards his own success/desires</small>	Jn 4:34; 5:30; Jn 8:28-29
	Was filled with the Spirit (Word) <small>Not the world's wisdom/ways</small>	Lk 4:1, 14
	Gave the gospel to others <small>Not temporary pleasures or relief</small>	Mk 1:14-15; Jn 3–4
	Lived a holy, obedient life <small>Not sinful</small>	1 Pt 2:22; Phil 2:8
Love/Understanding	Sought to meet needs of others <small>Not uncaring/self-focused</small>	Mt 4:23; Lk 4:18-21
	Sacrificed self and own desires <small>Not self-preserving/selfish</small>	Lk 22:42; Phil 2:6-8
	Was gentle whenever possible <small>Not harsh/demanding</small>	Mt 11:29; Jn 21:15-19
Zeal/Courage/Confidence (because of God and His promises)	Led the disciples and others <small>Not a follower when he shouldn't be</small>	Lk 9:6; Jn 6:2
	Showed initiative when He should have <small>Not waiting for someone else</small>	Mk 6:34-44; Lk 6:12-16
	Confronted when necessary <small>Not a compromiser/man-pleaser</small>	Mt 23:1-36; Mk 11:15-18
	Was decisive according to God's revealed will <small>Not wishy-washy or afraid</small>	Mt 4:1-11; Mk 8:31-38
Conscientiousness	Fulfilled responsibilities <small>Not irresponsible</small>	Jn 17:4; Jn 19:30
	Was diligent <small>Not lazy or a quitter</small>	Jn 5:17; Heb 12:2-3
Humility	Served and listened to others in His leadership <small>Not proudly lording it over others</small>	Jn 13:12-17; Jn 6:5-10
	Glorified another (the Father) <small>Not greedy for attention or recognition</small>	Jn 8:50,54; Jn 17:1,4

15

God's will for men is to put on Christlikeness (Romans 13:14). One cannot be a *real man* unless he is increasing in His qualities. Men should pray about them regularly and seek to emulate them in daily living (2 Peter 3:18).

Characteristics Drawn from the Qualifications of Male Leadership in the Church

More insight can be gained into God's expectations about masculinity by examining what God has said concerning male leadership in the church. In the Scriptures, we find two very precise lists of positive and negative qualities by which leaders are to be measured: 1Timothy 3:2-7 and Titus 1:6-9. Although Paul, in these passages, correlates this set of characteristics with church leadership, these qualities (except for *able to teach* and *not a new believer*) are addressed elsewhere in God's Word for the non-elder Christian. The instructions were given to insure that male leaders were habitually the kind of men that God wants *every* man to be. Because a leader is always some sort of example (good or bad), it is very important to God that every male leader reflect Christ (1 Corinthians 11:1). Therefore, since these two passages were specifically given by God to men, the basic instructions found in them are profitable for understanding what is truly masculine and what is not. It could even be said, from God's perspective, that these commands and prohibitions are prerequisites to genuine *manliness*.

Examining the qualities for godly spiritual leaders helps to further refine what it means to be a man. When defining masculinity, it is futile to be concerned with qualities that should be distinctly different from feminine counterparts, unless one has first thought about the more foundational traits of manhood. Hopefully, it has been made clear that one cannot be truly masculine by centering only on a few distinctive characteristics. Let us now direct our attention to those qualities directly related to man's unique, God-given role.

Role Characteristics in Which a Man Must Excel

By exploring God's intention concerning gender roles it becomes clear how a man should differ from a woman. Here is the key to distinctive masculine qualities. By understanding from

Scripture what God intended for a man to *do*, it is much easier to determine what characteristics must be emphasized. In this process, it will become obvious that women may also be expected to possess these qualities to some extent or in certain situations. But a man must excel in them in order to fulfill his major roles. This concept is very similar to spiritual gifts. For example, all Christians are commanded to evangelize and to be hospitable. However, some have been given the gift of evangelism or hospitality, and therefore will *excel* in that ability so that they might fulfill their role in the body of Christ. A strong and godly man will be characterized by the following qualities that are necessary to fulfill the roles that God has given to him.

Leadership

When God placed man in the Garden, He gave him specific instructions. Adam was to care for the Garden; to oversee it (Genesis 2:15). He was given charge of it even though God could have done a much better job Himself. Adam also had dominion over and named the animals (Genesis 1:28-30; 2:20). He was given these tasks before Eve came on the scene. When God placed Eve in the Garden, He made it clear that she was to assist Adam in the work he had been given to do. She was to be his helper (Genesis 2:18). God didn't say, "Here Eve, you take this half and Adam, you take the other." Adam was to lead; Eve was to help and follow.

Later in Scripture, husbands are clearly instructed to be the head in the marriage relationship, and women are commanded to submit to the husband's leadership and respect his God-given position (Ephesians 5:22-33). It was to men that God gave leadership positions in the nation of Israel. Furthermore, it is to men that God gave the position of leadership in the church (1 Timothy 2:11-12). It is obvious that God has given man the role of ultimate leadership.

This says absolutely nothing (positive or negative) about a woman's capabilities or personal equality. God simply chose to give this role to the man. In any endeavor, there must be an ultimate leader. God chose and equipped Adam for this role. If leadership is a God-given role for men, then each man needs to find the way to lead. For some men, who did not develop leadership skills while growing up, or have habitually shied away from leadership, it will be necessary to develop leadership skills over time rather than incompetently try to lead in a full or total capacity. Granted, some men are gifted by God with exceptional leadership abilities to be a leader of leaders. If all Christian men were taught that it is *manly* to initiate and lead, there would not be such a lack of male leadership in the home and the church. In regard to teaching young boys leadership, Douglas Wilson writes,

> Our boys need to learn humility, and they also need to learn boldness and courage. The only way to accomplish this balance is through a grasp of who God is. Because we have ceased teaching that God is our Father, with the attributes of divine Father, we have lost an understanding of imitative masculinity. Because of this, our boys veer into one of two ditches. Either they embrace humility without boldness which in boys is effeminate, or they embrace boldness without humility which is destructive (Douglas Wilson, *Future Men*, Moscow, ID: Canon Press, 2001, p. 49).

The qualities that one must strongly possess in order to carry out a leadership role are: **wisdom, initiative, decisiveness, humility, courage, and personal involvement.**

Love (The 1 Corinthians 13 type)

At creation, Adam and Eve were given to each other as marital companions. This intention for marriage is further made clear later in Scripture (Malachi 2:14). Certainly, love is involved in this kind of companionship. In the New Testament, husbands are singled out as needing to exemplify the kind of sacrificial love that Christ has for the Church (Ephesians 5:25). They are also specifically commanded to live with their wives in an understanding way (1 Peter 3:7). Clearly, husbands are to excel in this love. Also, Christ commanded the men He left behind to love and serve one another (John 13:15). John Benton writes,

> There is need for repentance. Perhaps single men have used their strength they have to serve themselves rather than other people. Perhaps husbands have used their strength to dominate their wives and children. We need to learn to come back to God, back to his Word of Scripture, and learn again

18

to walk with him. To be a loving sacrificial servant of others, as Jesus Christ was, is not to be namby-pamby. It is to be a true man. (*Gender Questions*, London: Evangelical Press, 2000.)

A true man, then, will *excel* in qualities that show love, such as: giving, gentleness, consideration, kindness, servanthood, and self-sacrifice.

Protection

A natural outworking of the roles of leader and lover produces the role of protector. After the Fall, it certainly became part of Adam's job description to protect his wife. As the supreme leader and lover, God has made a commitment to protect believers (1 Thessalonians 3:3). A man must make the same commitment to protect his wife, his children, and his church. Though God in His love does not always protect people from the consequences of their sin or every evil in the world, His protection definitely involves both *physical* and *spiritual* aspects, just like a husband's love.

In the Old Testament, men made up the army to protect cities, women, and children (Numbers 1:2-3). In 1 Corinthians 16:13, God commanded the brethren of the Corinthian church to protect the faith (the Word of God) with the words "act like men", or be courageous! Christ certainly protected the disciples He loved and led (John 17:12). He also expected all the church leaders to protect the body of Christ (Acts 20:28). Being manly involves protecting.

The qualities a man must clearly possess before he will be a good protector are: **courage, boldness, strength (both physical and spiritual) and watchfulness.**

Provider

The roles of leader and lover automatically encompass the idea of *provision*. God, as the one who leads and loves, also provides for every true need (Psalm 34:10). Husbands and fathers are specifically given the role of provider in the New Testament (Ephesians 5:29; 1 Timothy 5:8). Leaders of God's people are given this role as well (Ezekiel 34:1-4; John 21:15-17). Men should seek to meet the true needs of those whom God has placed in their care, whether physical or spiritual. In order to fulfill this role, a truly masculine man will abound in the characteristics of **diligence** (hard work!),

personal involvement, and **servanthood**. He will also do all that he can to acquire **a good job** which allows him to care well for those he must love and lead.

A man will be better able to fulfill God's intention as he puts off sin and grows in Christlikeness. There are many sins that will keep a man from possessing these qualities and fulfilling his God given roles. Some of them are: fear of man, pride, laziness, selfishness, idolatry (e.g., work, money, possessions, success, one's wife), and a lack of trust in God and His truth. A real man will, by God's grace, strive to put off these and any other sin that stands in the way of his masculinity. He will seek God's help to implement all of these godly (Christlike) qualities into his daily affairs. John Piper writes, "At the heart of mature masculinity is a sense of benevolent responsibility to lead, provide for and protect women in ways appropriate to a man's differing relationships"(John Piper *What's the Difference?* Wheaton, IL: Crossway Books, 1990 p. 22).

The extent to which these role qualities are present in a man's life determines how well he displays these distinguishing aspects of his masculinity. He should surpass his counterpart in them. Furthermore, he has the freedom to exercise them with both of the genders. Women, on the other hand, may *at times* need to assume these roles with children, other women and men outside the realm of the church, but she will find true identity and satisfaction if she is *more* characterized by the role of assistant or helper, so far as marriage and spiritual instruction are concerned (1 Timothy 2:12).

Furthermore, a woman in the work place must be able to deal with a man under her position in a way that preserves his masculinity and her femininity. Though many women have found a certain fleshly satisfaction in leading, they are surely missing a far more pure and holy satisfaction that is found only in fulfilling the roles that God has given her.

Similarly, if men were to be more consistent in living out these role qualities they would not be inclined to strive toward counterfeit expressions of masculinity such as machismo or authoritarianism. Men of this persuasion have fallen into one kind of unbiblical extreme. The other extreme, of course, is that of passive or effeminate men. If a man overly focuses on any one of the characteristics described in this booklet, it will cause him to err toward one extreme or the other, to be unmanly, and sin in his duties and relationships. Instead, a man must fully embrace God's superior design for the sexes. About this, John MacArthur observes, "They are perfect complements – one the head, leader, and provider; the other the helper, supporter, and companion."

The Bottom Line

So what does it mean to be a *real man*? It means not to trust in one's own judgment about masculinity but, instead, to cling to the fact there *are* absolutes outlined in the Word of God. It means to understand the basic characteristics of mankind and recognize that there should be a difference between the genders. It means possessing saving faith in and a likeness to the person of Christ. It means striving to emulate the qualities that God outlines for godly men in the church. Finally, it means to *capitalize* on the specific qualities that are needed to fulfill our God-given roles. In short, it means to live out a biblical worldview of masculinity.

Boys need to be taught the characteristics of biblical manhood by parents and other spiritual teachers. Furthermore, these are qualities that should be presented to the male population in all Bible-believing churches and institutions. Christian men need to take personal responsibility to study Scriptural teaching in this area, communicating with other godly men about it, reading some of the resources below, and depending on God's grace to change.

Though many of the masculine qualities discussed here are related to the husband, Scripture also presents them as pertaining to single men who are God's servants. Therefore, these truths are for each and every man, single or married, young or old. All men should fervently seek to pursue a true and life-changing understanding of the basic characteristics of man and Christ, take to heart specific biblical charges to men, and look for opportunities to lead, love, protect, and provide. Then, he will be *a real man*.

> **Masculinity (mas-kyoo-lin-i-ty)**: The possession and pursuit of redeemed perspective and character, enhanced by qualities consistent with the distinguishing male roles of leading, loving, protecting, and providing—all for the glory of God.

Read it

Chapter Three
THE BASIS FOR BIBLICAL MANHOOD IN MARRIAGE
Understanding the Husband's Role

One arena where the rubber meets the road concerning our "big three" is that of marriage. In this chapter we will seek to gain a fuller understanding of the husband's role and explore how it correlates to the wife's role. This will help us see how the married man can flesh out the three Christ-like qualities of masculinity, leadership and decision making. It is through his God-given role that the saved husband exemplifies Christ and becomes God's kind of man to his wife, his family, and the world. As we outline and apply the husband's role, we will revisit God's perspective of man and woman, some of the role characteristics and the godly (leadership) qualities mentioned earlier, but from a different perspective. It will become clear, that for some of these traits, there is actually multiple scriptural mandates. They are mentioned in different contexts of a man's life. This is because they are that vital for the "real man!"

As Creator and ruler of this world and everything in it, God is the one who has the perfect plan for marriage. We must accept His plan and depend on His infinite wisdom concerning the roles of both husband and wife. In this booklet we will seek only to gain a basic understanding of the husband's role, exploring how it correlates to the wife's role. This biblical perspective is needed for Christ-likeness in marriage. It is through his role that the husband exemplifies Christ to his wife, his family, and the world. Obviously, before this will happen a husband must have a truly changed heart (salvation) and he must also know how in the world he can practically change.

In this century our society has managed to confuse thoroughly the roles of husband and wife. Even many "Christians" have taken the viewpoint that it is okay for everyone to do what is right in their own eyes. This individualistic mindset has historically brought heartache to God's people and shame to God's name (Proverbs 18:1-2; Isaiah 5:21). The exemplary husband must see the importance of doing things God's way. For the husband to truly understand God's way he must first understand God's perspective of man and woman.

God's Perspective of Man and Woman

There are varied views about the nature of man and woman. Some say they are equal, while others say they are not. Both the authoritarian man and the feminist woman have muddied the waters concerning the issue of equality. As Creator, God has the right view about their nature and equality. In actuality, they are both equal and unequal, depending on what aspect of their lives is being considered.

1. The two are *positionally* and *personally equal.*

Both man and woman were created in the image of God. This means that each was created with the ability and responsibility to know and glorify God. It also means that both genders were created the same in nature and intellect. Neither gender is viewed, loved, or accepted by God more or less. From God's perspective they are equal in essence and standing.

> **God created man in His own image, in the image of God He created him; male and female He created them.**
> **Genesis 1:27**

> **There is neither Jew nor Greek, there is neither slave nor free man, there is neither male nor female; for you are all one in Christ Jesus.**
> **Galatians 3:28**

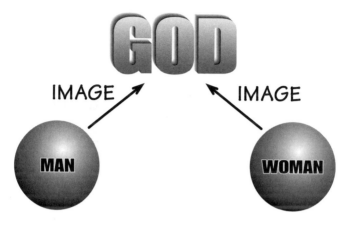

2. The two are functionally unequal.

As with the Trinity, there is to be an order of function between the husband and wife. God has wisely assigned who gets which function. This delegation of function has nothing to do with worth or ability. It has everything, however, to do with love, humility, and the goal of effectively glorifying God. The husband is given authority over the wife and the wife is to submit to the husband's leadership because this can best glorify God. Since the goal of every sincere Christian is to glorify God, the husband and wife can each accept their role with joy.

The husband and wife are unequal only in *authority*. This is in keeping with the rest of life, is it not? Parents are in authority over children, the government is in authority over citizens, employers are in authority over employees, church leadership is in authority over church members, and so on. A good question is, "Why all the difficulty surrounding the authority of the husband?"

The Godhead has no problem with the right view of submission or the abuse of authority. They have perfect unity and contentment. So, the answer to our previous question is: "Our difficulties with authority and/or submission come from our own sinful pride." The husband must humble himself to realize that he does not have unlimited authority, (it is delegated authority), that his authority is not for his own benefit, and that his authority should be carried out lovingly. A wife must humble herself to realize that she obeys Christ by respecting her husband's position at all times even when she does not agree to sin or must deal with the husband's sin.

Both leadership and submission should also flow out of a love relationship between the husband and wife. Alexander Strauch writes in his book, *Men and Women, Equal Yet Different*:

> The husband-wife relationship is not a boss-employee, a commander-soldier, or a teacher-student relationship. It is a love relationship in which two adults become united as one. Within this union, one partner lovingly takes the lead and the other willingly and actively supports that lead (Lewis and Roth Publishers, 1999, p. 23).

As Ephesians 5:22-24 explains, the functional roles of the husband and wife should be patterned after that of Christ and the Church. The pattern is also explained later in 1 Corinthians.

But I want you to understand that Christ is the head of every man, and the man is the head of a woman, and God is the head of Christ.
1 Corinthians 11:3

With the delegation of authority comes glory. A person in authority receives a certain amount of glory or prominence by virtue of his position and the submission of those under him. In this sense, woman is the glory of man and man is the glory of God. The husband must keep in mind that he is in this place of glory by no merit of his own and that he should "pass on" all glory to God. Men, be reminded that God caused King Herod to be eaten by worms when he kept glory for himself (Acts 12:20-23).

There are some who suggest there should be a mutual submission between husband and wife. Naturally, there is a sense in which both husband and wife are to lay down their own wills and give preference to one another. Certainly a husband is to take into account (and whenever he deems appropriate and possible, *act upon*) his wife's requests, counsel and admonitions. However, there should never be a time when the wife takes the position of authority over the husband. The favorite (and only) passage that proponents of mutual submission site is Ephesians 5:21. However,

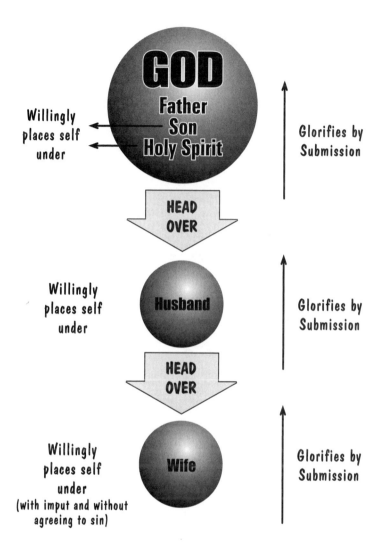

the meaning and context of "one another" in this verse does not support their view, nor does it negate the several times that God commands the wife to be in subjection to her husband (Ephesians 5:22; Colossians 3:18; 1 Peter 3:1; Titus 2:4-5). Based upon the context, a better rendering of "one another," is "some to others." Then the Apostle Paul proceeds to develop the "some to others" in the remaining verses.

A Husband's Role Specifically Involves Leadership and Decision Making

We have already established that the husband is head over the wife and his family. We have also established that he is to lead as Christ leads the Church (Ephesians 5:23; 1 Corinthians 11:3). What do these things actually mean in a practical sense in the marriage? We can see some of the specifics from our Ephesians 5:22-33 passage.

The Pattern of Ephesians Five			
Christ/Husband		**Church/Wife**	
:22-24,30	Presides as Head Leads by example and direct input Is responsible for decisions	:22,24	Follows as a respectful submissive one
:25,28,33	Pursues to actively love (sacrificially giving his own life for her) includes 'protecting' and 'cherishing'	:24,33	Honors and serves Christ's/husband's righteous goals
:29	Provides physically and spiritually— includes 'nourishes'	:29,30	Depends on, looks to, wisely uses resources to give back and serve

Christ is the perfect picture of leadership in this passage. One who follows him must know when and how to make godly, wise decisions. This just comes with the territory of leadership! God's kind of man and husband cannot shy away from decisions, abuse the decision-making privilege or make decisions mystically. We will discuss decision-making in detail in chapter 6.

A Husband's Role Specifically Involves Loving

The command for husbands to love their wives is repeated several times in Scripture. Obviously this is to be a major aspect of the husband's role. His wife bears the responsibility to love him as a person (friend or foe—Matthew 5:44; 22:39), as a believer (1 John 4:7), and as a spouse (Titus 2:4). But we as husbands have been told specifically four times to love our wives! We must seek to love her as a person, as a believer (if she is one), and as our spouse. Then, on top of this three-fold responsibility to love, we are given the command to love our wives as Christ loved the Church.

Husbands, love your wives, just as Christ also loved the church and gave Himself up for her.
Ephesians 5:25

So husbands ought also to love their own wives as their own bodies. He who loves his own wife loves himself; for no one ever hated his own flesh, but nourishes and cherishes it, just as Christ also does the church.
Ephesians 5:28-29

An exemplary husband is to love his wife:

• **Actively**

He must show his love in tangible ways. He will not simply *say*, "I love you," but he will assure her of his love by his deeds. It is also important that he refrain from pointing backwards to isolated demonstrations of love as if they are *frozen in time* and sufficient for *today*. He must continue to display his love daily. (1 Corinthians 13:4-8; Ephesians 5:25-33).

• **According to knowledge**

He will take the time and make the effort to know the best way to love her. *Understanding* her and her circumstances well will help him love her better. Another way he can love her according to knowledge is to *study* and *apply* God's kind of love and God's principles of marriage to his relationship with his wife. It is a lack of love for God and one's wife that causes a husband to say, "I don't like to read," "It's just not me to study," or "I can't take the time to read or become knowledgeable." I venture to say that if a man were offered a million dollars to study God's principles of marriage or to attend a marriage conference, he would make a great effort to make it happen (1 Peter 3:7).

• **Sacrificially**

He must put his wife before himself and serve her, even when it means a personal sacrifice on his part. Christ sacrificially loved us to the point of death. Our goal is to model our love after that of Christ. We must be willing to lay our lives down for our wife daily. A wife who is sacrificially loved will usually have no doubt of her husband's love (Ephesians 5:25).

There is a great deal of confusion surrounding the roles involved in marriage. It can be difficult to understand how the multiple authorities (the Lord, church leaders and husbands), relationships (with the Lord, with each other as spouses, fellow believers), and responsibilities (companionship, leadership, submission, etc.) all fit together. When we are trying to sort it all out we have to keep all of the relationships involved in mind. We could picture the marriage roles in this way:

Ephesians

Husband	Wife
Role: Child of God	Role: Child of God
Relationship: Fellow Disciple	Relationship: Fellow Disciple
Responsibilities: Walk with God	Responsibilities: Walk with God
Role: Brother	Role: Sister
Relationship: Members of One Another	Relationship: Members of One Another
Responsibilities: Mutual Sanctification Loving Attitude	Responsibilities: Mutual Sanctification Submissive Attitude
Role: Husband	Role: Wife
Relationship: One Flesh	Relationship: One Flesh
Responsibilities: Lead, Love, Pursue Oneness	Responsibilities: Submit, Assist, Pursue Oneness

What About You?

Now that we have taken a good look at the Bible concerning the role of husbands, it is time to compare yourself to it. Are you wholeheartedly ready and willing to take up the role that God has laid out for you? If so, you are desirous to be a better leader and a better lover. If you're not quite sure how to grow in these areas, there will be some practical helps to come in later chapters. The first step is for you to adopt God's viewpoint of your role as a husband.

Most likely you have become aware of some area of your role that needs restructuring. If this is true, confess it to the Lord and to your spouse. Strive to live in light of your new understanding. Remember, an exemplary husband knows that he is not perfect but keeps Christ ever before him as his example.

Chapter Four
UNDERSTANDING LEADERSHIP IN MARRIAGE

A common expression, "Take me to your leader!" should not create confusion anywhere, but especially not within a Christian family. The husband's leadership is a mandate from God, and as such is a privilege and responsibility. Even if you are not a married man, it is good for you to know these things and many of the principles in this chapter can be used in any leadership context. That being said, let us now turn our attention to the skill and art of leading. In this chapter, we will discuss the origin and limits of our leadership in marriage and also examine the general characteristics of Christlike leadership. Christ's way of leading is very different from the worldly leadership we often see and the fleshly leadership that comes so naturally.

The Natural Man	The Spiritual Man
•Self-confident •Knows men •Makes own decisions •Ambitious •Originates own methods •Enjoys commanding others •Motivated by personal considerations •Independent	•Confident in God •Also knows God •Seeks to find God's will •Self-effacing [to erase self or make self inconspicuous] •Finds and follows God's methods •Delights to obey God •Motivated by love for God and man •God-dependent

Poor leadership is the cause of many conflicts in marriage. Any time a husband's method of leadership helps him to accomplish his own *fleshly gain*, enables him to *lord it over* his wife or allows him to be *irresponsible*, his method of leading is *wrong* (1Peter 5:2-3). Christlike leadership qualities are indispensable to the Christian husband's marriage.

The Husband Has God-Given Authority

The responsibility to lead always comes from holding a position of authority. "Headship" is bestowed by God on the husband at the time of the marriage vows. There are abuses and distortions of the privilege of leadership, however, because there are misunderstandings about the headship or authority the husband has been given by God. Following are some important aspects of the authority God has given the husband.

Your Authority Is Limited

Only God has unlimited authority. You are limited in your authority by the commands of God's Word, just as the authority of the government can go only so far. Even though all Christians are commanded to be in subjection to the government, the government's authority is limited. It only has the authority that God gives it. Its authority is not above God's. Paul makes this point well in Romans:

> **Every person is to be in subjection to the governing authorities. For there is no authority except from God, and those which exist are established by God. Therefore whoever resists authority has opposed the ordinance of God; and they who have opposed will receive condemnation upon themselves.**
> **Romans 13:1-2**

This same principle applies to the authority the husband has been given. Some husbands seem to think they have the authority to say anything, do anything, or require anything. A husband does *not* have the authority to sin or to ask his wife to sin. You are under God's authority and have been given a *measure* of authority to carry out God's revealed will. While it is true that your wife must obey you unless you ask her to sin, *your concern* must be that you are obeying God and loving your wife in whatever decisions and requests you make. God will hold you accountable for your leadership. We must honor God by using our authority in the way that He intended. Anytime a husband sees his authority over and above the ordained limits, or without God's other very important commands, he will be a poor leader. He will not be leading in the way a Christian husband should.

Your Authority Must Be Active

You need to remember that your authority requires you to lead. It is not an option. God has made this very clear:

For the husband is the head of the wife, as Christ also is the head of the church, He Himself being the Savior of the body. But as the church is subject to Christ, so also the wives ought to be to their husbands in everything.
Ephesians 5:23-24

God is a God of order. Chaos, confusion, and disorganization should not be present in anything that God has designed or instituted. In His wisdom, God knows that order is necessary to accomplish a purpose. He has required order in the way that creation functions (Genesis 1-2), in the way that the nation of Israel functioned (Exodus 35-Numbers 9), in the way that the family should function (1 Corinthians 11:3; Ephesians 6:1), in the way that the Church should function (1 Corinthians 14:40), and so on. We have even seen that there is order in how the Godhead (Father, Son, Holy Spirit) itself operates. I believe it is obvious that one reason God has given you your authority is to put order in the institution of marriage, so that His purposes might be accomplished (Ephesians 5:21-33; Colossians 3:18-4:1).

Some purposes for the authority you have been given are:

- To help others see how God leads his people
- To develop humility and obedience in all those concerned
- To guide the family in righteousness

- To give a sense of order and stability in the home
- To provide what is needed for the family
- To protect the family
- To accomplish ministry for God more effectively
- To help the family be a good witness to the world

All for
God's
glory

God has given you your authority *to use.* He will, one day, hold you responsible for your faithfulness in this area. Are you above reproach before God and man in this area? In Paul's instructions to Timothy, he writes that overseers and deacons must be men who are "above reproach" even in how they manage their home (1 Timothy 3:2, 10). Paul then goes on to explain *how* a man is to be" above reproach." In his list of ways he says:

> ... **Not addicted to wine or pugnacious, but gentle, peaceable, free from the love of money. He must be** *one who manages his own household well,* **keeping his children under control with all dignity (but if a man** *does not know how to manage his own household,* **how will he take care of the church of God?). Deacons must be husbands of only one wife, and** *good managers of their children and their own households.*
> **1 Timothy 3:3-5, 12 [emphasis mine]**

In these verses the word "manage" (*prohistemi*) means "to lead and care for." If you want to be a man who is "above reproach" or "blameless" (NKJV), you must lead and care for your home well.

The Husband is a Type of Shepherd-Leader

In the Scriptures, God is pictured as the Shepherd of Israel (Psalm 80:1; Isaiah 40:11). He cared for them as He led them. He always knew the direction that He wanted His people to go, but He exercised great patience along the way. He often allowed His people to serve Him with their own talents and goals, but He also had boundaries that He decisively required them to stay within (e.g., Joshua 1:7). Christ referred to Himself as "The Good Shepherd" and was the perfect human example of leadership (John 10:11). Even though our God has all power and authority, He always leads His people like a shepherd:

> **"I am the good shepherd, and I know My own and My own know Me."**
> **John 10:14**

Since our goal is to be like Christ, and if Christ is a shepherd to those He leads, then we need to be caring to those we lead also (1 John 2:6). As much as possible, our leadership needs to have similar qualities as the shepherding done by God, and more specifically, the shepherding done by Christ.

The word *shepherd* brings our leadership into perspective. We are not kings, high above our wives, but actually lowly under-shepherds, doing the bidding of the Chief Shepherd. Yes, we do have authority to make decisions, but *authority is not the goal*. Authority is a means to an end—God's end. It is the means by which we care for our wives and do God's will. Furthermore, it is only one aspect of our relationship with our wives. We are also partners and companions. Most men dwell on their authority too much. Authority is something that you exercise when you have to. I've heard it said that our perspective should not be that we love to rule, but that we rule to love. Shepherding, on the other hand, is something you should always have in the forefront of your mind because it implies complete and daily care, whatever that may entail. Let's take a closer look at the qualities of a shepherd by looking at God's shepherding and His instructions to under-shepherds of God's people.

1. A shepherd knows where he is going.

> **"For I have come down from heaven, not to do my own will, but the will of Him who sent me."**
> **John 6:38**

A shepherd must know his destination before he can lead his flock there. Christ certainly knew where He was going. He was intent on glorifying God, and He used perfect wisdom in all His decisions.

A shepherd is neither "wishy-washy" nor rash in his decisions. In order to lead, he must be decisive, but very carefully decisive. A shepherd will always be in the process of making informed and purposeful decisions in order to care for his sheep properly. He needs to be aware of the circumstances, dangers and possibilities around his sheep, as much as possible. He also needs to know his sheep well. Being decisive does not mean that the shepherd will *always* be making and expressing decisions, but that he will always be thinking, studying, and evaluating.

> **He who gives an answer before he hears, it is folly and shame to him....The mind of the prudent acquires knowledge, and the ear of the wise seeks knowledge.**
> **Proverbs 18:13, 15**

Obviously we cannot be lazy as husbands. We must not sit back and let our wives do the evaluating and the decision-making. We should certainly enlist their input, but the evaluating and the decision-making are *our own* responsibility.

Wisdom comes from the Word of God. Husband, there is no way for you to lead your wife in the ways of God and in a wise way in this world unless you, yourself, are fixed on God's truth. You must pursue knowing God's Person, goals, and ways (through His Word) with fervor. You must devote yourself to this. A man who wants to prosper in the will of God will do what God told Joshua to do:

> **"This book of the law shall not depart from your mouth, but you shall meditate on it day and night, so that you may be careful to do according to all that is written in it; for then you will make your way prosperous, and then you will have success."**
> **Joshua 1:8**

2. A shepherd knows how to lead lovingly.

> **"The Lord is my shepherd... Surely goodness and lovingkindness shall follow me all the days of my life...."**
> **Psalm 23:1,6**

As Psalm 23 indicates, God (our Shepherd) is always bringing about good for His sheep and showing lovingkindness. A true shepherd loves and cares for his sheep at all times. In John 10:1-16, Jesus contrasts a true shepherd with a hireling. The true shepherd is willing to give his life for the sheep. The hireling is not. The true shepherd knows his sheep well. The hireling does not. A hireling looks after the sheep because he is paid to look after them. A true shepherd looks after the sheep because they belong to him and he cares for them.

3.   A shepherd leads by example.

> **"When he [the shepherd of the sheep] puts forth his own, he goes before them..."**
> **John 10:4a**

A shepherd leads by example, first and foremost. He may have times when he has to use a different method, but most of the time he goes before the sheep and the sheep follow him. Christ led by example while He was here on earth. He led the disciples to pray by example (Matthew 6: 5-15). He led them to serve one another by example (John 13:3-15). He taught them how to do ministry by example before He sent them out to minister on their own (Luke 8:1-9:6).

Likewise we need to be leading our wives by example. The motto, "Do as I say, not as I do" will not satisfy God or your wife. No one wants to follow a hypocrite. How we live speaks more loudly than our words. I am convinced that some of us need to do much less talking and a great deal more living!

God clearly outlined what a man who leads by example looks like in his instruction to the church on choosing godly men for service. The virtues listed in 1 Timothy 3:1-3 and Titus 1:5-9 are prerequisites for church leadership because they are exemplary characteristics. Except for two that are specific to a church leadership role, (able to teach and not a new convert), these qualities are ones that all men should possess.

Characteristics of the Godly Man	
Above reproach	He is blameless because he does not practice evil. If and when he is accused, there is no evidence.
Husband of one wife	He is a one-woman man. He is faithful and true to his wife.
Temperate	He is in control of himself and well-composed.
Prudent	He is in touch with reality and alert. He has sound judgement.
Respectable	He is proper, orderly and modest, as opposed to scatter-brained and immature.
Hospitable	He is a friend to strangers and willing to have others in his home.
Not addicted to much wine	He is moderate and self-controlled. He is not a drunkard.
Not pugnatious/ Uncontentious	He is not quarrelsome or easily angered.
Free from the love of money	He is not covetous or focused on earthly wealth.
Manages his household well	He maintains and cares for his house well. He leads his family, rather than driving them or letting them rule him.
Keeps his children under control with all dignity	He has children who obey him. Because he is dignified in how he manages them, they act with dignity.

4. A shepherd knows how to oversee.

> **The Word of the Lord came to me saying, "Son of man, prophesy against the shepherds of Israel. Prophesy and say to those shepherds, 'Thus says the Lord God, "Woe, shepherds of Israel ...** *with force and with severity you have dominated them* **[God's sheep].""**
> **Ezekiel 34:1-4** [emphasis and explanation mine]

Shepherding is not a harsh, driving or controlling kind of leadership. Some men treat their wives like little children, doing everything for them or trying to control their every activity and decision. A shepherding husband, however, does not "lord it over" his wife. There is most of the time a significant measure of freedom in the way a good shepherd leads. He takes those under him in a certain direction; he does not seek to scrutinize and control their every step. Be careful that your leadership is largely oversight and not a matter of control.

A husband who lords it over his wife does not really care for her as he should, but instead cares most about his own agenda. This kind of husband might also look down on others and have difficulty believing that they are capable (by God's grace) of doing what they need to do and becoming what they need to become. He may be tempted to see himself as the only one who must make everything happen, instead of giving others a chance and trusting God to work. He also is usually lacking in personal and relational skills and the ability to recognize his own sin and shortcomings. As an exemplary husband, we must put off any "lording it over" tendencies, and put on patience, self-control, and humility.

> **Shepherd the flock of God among you, exercising oversight not under compulsion,...nor yet as lording it over those allotted to your charge, but proving to be examples to the flock.**
> **1 Peter 5:2-3**

5. A shepherd is involved.

> **"I am the Good Shepherd ... I know my own and my own know Me."**
> **John 10:14**

A number of husbands are too cowardly, fearful, or busy about the wrong things to be involved. Some fear the reaction of their wife and the consequences of doing the right thing. Instead, they must have courage, faith in God, and trust that His Word will guide them in whatever results from taking the responsibility to lead. Overly busy husbands do not yet grasp that they will be held accountable for their contribution (or the lack thereof) to the state of the home. In the same way that church leaders will be held responsible for the care of their flock, you will be held responsible for the care of your home flock.

6. A shepherd is diligent in his responsibility.

Shepherd the flock ... with eagerness.
1 Peter 5:2

It is very easy to rationalize away our responsibility as husbands. I've heard (and used myself) the best of excuses: "I'm too tired." "I'm too busy." "I'm not wired that way." "That's not my style." "That's just too much to expect of me right now." The common denominators in all of these excuses is selfishness (Philippians 2:3-4). Christ, however, is never self-focused or lazy in His care for us. A good shepherd is diligent and eager to care for his sheep. We must, therefore, be diligent and eager in our leadership as well.

If you have been letting your wife lead, you need to sit down with her and express your intention to love her and God by leading as you should. Tell her of your desire to lovingly lead without lording it over her. Discuss specific ways that she can better follow you. Once you both have the same goal of obeying God in this area, you both need to be gracious and patient as you learn new habits.

7. A shepherd protects.

I am the good shepherd; the good shepherd lays
down His life for the sheep. He who is the hired
hand and not a shepherd ... flees because he is a
hired hand and is not concerned about the sheep.
John 10:11-13

A shepherd is always on the lookout for danger and is ready to intervene. Certainly, he would never intentionally or knowingly put his sheep in harm's way. As husbands we need to do what we can to keep our wives safe from danger. If at all possible, we need to be with them, or see that someone is, when there is potential danger. We should do what we can to give them a safe place to live and a reliable car to drive. We also need to be on the lookout for any spiritual dangers such as heresies, known temptations, and excessive worldly input (i.e. the wrong kind of television shows, novels, friendships, etc.). It is never right for a husband to know-ingly allow his wife to be in any kind of preventable danger.

8.   A shepherd provides.

> **The Lord is my shepherd, I shall not want [be in true need].**
> **Psalm 23:1 [explanation mine]**

Christ, as the Good Shepherd, provides for His Church. He cares for her every need, and makes the well-being of His flock His concern. Providing for our wives is an important part of loving our wives the way Christ loves us. The Bible is clear that we must care for the physical and spiritual needs of our wives (1 Timothy 5:8). To fulfill our responsibility we must provide food, clothing, shelter, rest, healthcare, and sexual satisfaction, as well as a good church and spiritual oversight.

9.   A shepherd instructs.

> **The Lord is my shepherd . . . . He guides me in the paths of righteousness for His name's sake.**
> **Psalm 23:1-3**

With the understanding that our instruction must be balanced by the oversight principle (see number 5), we must be sure to *give instruction*, especially in the things of God. A shepherd doesn't just let the sheep wander *anywhere without any instruction*. Taking the time to study with, review sermons with, or have devotions with your wife is a good way to lead by instruction. Having a special time to discuss concerns and decisions is also very helpful.

10.   A shepherd corrects.

> **The Lord is my Shepherd.... Your rod and Your staff, they comfort me.**
> **Psalm 23:1,4**

Out of love, a shepherd will occasionally have to correct a way-ward lamb. He does this for the well-being of the sheep. Even though correction may not be pleasant, it can still be the best thing for a lamb. It may even be a comforting thing for a lamb to know his shepherd will not let him stray and that his shepherd truly cares. Sometimes a wife may need to be clearly corrected with God's staff (the Word of God). This should be done only when there is clear sin involved and for the purpose of helping her and glorifying God. You need to ascertain whether she is *weak, fainthearted* or *unruly* and respond accordingly (1 Thessalonians 5:14). Most wives who are lovingly led by their husbands rarely need anything more than a loving admonition.

Sometimes a lamb does not learn from correction, but continues to stray. A shepherd of literal sheep will do whatever is necessary to help the sheep learn what is best for them. As humans, our authority stops short of physically abusing our wives! Men, we are absolutely NEVER allowed to strike or harm our wives. Any husband who hurts his wife physically is committing a serious moral offense before God (1 Timothy 3:3). He is also committing a criminal offense and should suffer the legal consequences. Doing physical harm to your wife also will have the devastating result of breaking a trust that is difficult to regain. If you and your wife are in this position, it would be wise to seek godly counsel to restore the relationship and to gain accountability.

There may be a time when our wife needs more than *our own* correction with God's Word. After we have led by example, have given instruction, have gently admonished, and, finally, have firmly rebuked in love—all to no avail, a more drastic measure may be needed before the wife will submit to the will of God. The Lord has told us what to do in this kind of situation. If she is a professing believer, we are to bring in another believer and the whole church if necessary (Luke 17:3-4; Matthew 18:15-20).

11.   A shepherd seeks to restore his sheep.

The Lord is my shepherd .... He restores my soul.
Psalm 23:1, 3

**Brethren, even if anyone is caught in any trespass,
you who are spiritual, *restore such a one* in a spirit
of gentleness; each one looking to yourself, so that
you too will not be tempted.**
Galatians 6:1 [emphasis mine]

Whether a lamb is hurt in the process of following or of rebelling, a good shepherd seeks to restore that sheep to full health. A shepherd will compassionately receive and help the lamb that is willing to receive help. In the same way, we must be willing to forgive and/or assist a hurting wife. It is important that you seek to really understand your wife as you are trying to restore her. I would strongly suggest that you run the risk of erring on the side of comfort, until it becomes evident that your wife needs more.

The Husband is a Servant-Leader

To some a servant leader may seem like an irreconcilable paradox (opposites that cannot be put together). But actually, the two concepts must go hand in hand. Christ was the perfect leader and yet He was very much the perfect servant.

> **"It is not this way among you, but whoever wishes to become great among you shall be your servant, and whoever wishes to be first among you shall be your slave; just as the Son of Man did not come to be served, but to serve, and to give His life a ransom for many."**
> **Matthew 20:26-28**

Serving does not lessen one's authority or leadership. Instead, it enhances it—especially the leading-by-example aspect. One who leads as Christ leads is always thinking of others, not self. He is willing to sacrifice his own comfort and even his own well-being for those he leads. He is willing to put himself last, prefer others, and even serve those he leads. Christ gave us an amazing example of serving when He humbled himself and served the disciples in the upper room:

> **"You call Me Teacher and Lord; and you are right, for so I am. If I then, the Lord and the Teacher, washed your feet, you also ought to wash one another's feet. For I gave you an example that you also should do as I did to you. Truly, truly, I say to you, a slave is not greater than his master, nor**

> **is one who is sent greater than the one who sent him. If you know these things, you are blessed if you do them."**
>
> **John 13:13-17**

Jesus' message to the disciples was loud and clear. If He was willing to be a servant, we certainly should be too. Husbands, how do you serve your wife? Even though she is called to assist you, you must serve her. A servant will be more concerned about his own responsibility than that of others. First be sure that you are serving your wife, then address her need to assist you if she is not doing her part. The greatest leader of all time was a servant-leader.

With God All Things Are Possible

Christ has left you with the perfect example of leadership. Though it is not humanly possible, God is able to make you into the leader you should be. Change will take humble and prayerful dependence on Him. Confess and repent of any sin in the area of your leadership to both God and your wife. Begin to make this aspect of your marriage a serious matter of prayer. Pinpoint where your leadership goes wrong and seek to put on right thinking and actions instead. As you seek to honor God as a shepherd and servant-leader, you will be better able to exemplify Christ.

Chapter Five
LEADERSHIP SPECIFICS IN MARRIAGE

Know Your Own Goals

Whether you are a leader of a household or not, you must first determine your personal and spiritual goals before you can lead others. What are your educational and vocational goals? What are your ministry goals? You should not aimlessly drift from day to day taking things as they come. Furthermore, every man needs to know the importance of knowing what his own goals in marriage should be. It is critical for us to know where we are headed and make plans. As we do this, we must also remember that all of those goals and plans are subject to God's will and Sovereign providence (James 4:13-15, Proverbs 16:9).

After you have set your own personal course, you are ready to think about the direction and goals having to do with your household. When you are considering direction and goals for your household, be bibically-controlled and balanced, and be *sure* to involve your wife.

Remember that you are to be *one* with her and she is to be your *helper*. Most likely, she will be of great assistance.

Direction and possible goals you can establish for your household:

- Establish the Word of God as the standard for your home.
- Establish how you will provide for your family spiritually (a good church and biblical instruction).
- Establish how you will work toward financial stability and providing basic needs for the family (for both immediate and extended family).
- Establish operational guidelines for your own household, (devotions, family meetings, phone use [especially for teens], family nights, bedtimes, noise level, neatness standard, etc.).

- Establish ministry goals and guidelines for you and your family (the need for ministry, how often outside ministry takes place, how you can minister together, hospitality frequency, etc.).
- Be careful not to have some inflexible schedule that is never modified

Know the Areas to Oversee

I believe we can safely (scripturally) say that we should oversee any area of our wife's life that affects her well-being (spiritual and otherwise), the lives of the other family members, the management of the home, and the family's witness of God before a watching world. An observant overseer will see areas where the Lord might already be working in his wife's life and look for ways to be of assistance in that area. (See Appendix II for Leadership Worksheets).

Areas to oversee:

1. Her spiritual welfare

> **Husbands, love your wives, just as Christ also loved the church and gave Himself up for her, so that He might sanctify her, having cleansed her by the washing of water with the word, that He might present to Himself the church in all her glory, having no spot or wrinkle or any such thing; but that she should be holy and blameless.**
> **Ephesians 5:25-27**

- See that you pray for her and with her.
- Provide for her to be a part of, and involved with, your local church, if she is a believer.
- Be sure that you are a good testimony to her by your life and that you share the gospel with her as you have opportunity, if she is unsaved.
- See that you do not take on the role and responsibility of the Holy Spirit by constantly admonishing her and trying to do a sanctifying work in her heart.

- See that you pray with her. How often and how long are not mandated by God, but praying with her daily is very helpful for your understanding of her concerns and for being one with her.
- See that you look into God's Word with her regularly. This can be done through devotions, review of sermon notes, a book, or a study. You can use this time to lead and instruct in spiritual matters. Recognize that she can contribute insight as well. Make sure that you focus most on your own response to God's Word. Also study with her when she has specific questions or needs. You can use your own study methods or a study done by someone else.

2. Her decision-making

> **For this reason also, since the day we heard of it, we have not ceased to pray for you and to ask that you may be filled with the knowledge of His will in all spiritual wisdom and understanding, so that you will walk in a manner worthy of the Lord, to please Him in all respects.**
> **Colossians 1:9-10**

- Encourage her toward the goal of glorifying God.
- Teach her about the two biggest pitfalls of good decision- making: selfishness and subjectivity (following one's feelings and one's own judgment, rather than God's Word).
- Encourage her to emphasize biblical principles in her decision-making.
- Help her to consider her priorities in her decision-making: God, husband, children, home, and the local church. This is not to be done in a strict order at every given moment.

3. Her relationships

> **Older women likewise are to be reverent in their behavior, not malicious gossips nor enslaved to much wine, teaching what is good, so that they may encourage the young women to love their husbands, to love their children, to be sensible, pure, workers at home, kind, being subject to**

> their own husbands, so that the word of God will
> not be dishonored.
> ### Titus 2:3-5

- Make sure she understands her relationship with you.
  - to be one
  - to be a companion
  - to be your helper
  - to be submissive and respectful. Make sure she knows how to give a godly appeal when she wants you to reconsider a decision, an action, or an attitude (see *The Excellent Wife*, by Martha Peace).
- See that she is protected from sinful or evil relationships. Come to her aid when she needs help in dealing with people who try to take advantage of her kindness, are unreasonable, or act inappropriately toward her.
- Help her to balance her relationship priorities: God, you, the children, and others.
- See that she has any help and resources she needs for her relationships: you, her children, her friends, her boss or co-workers, and her extended family.

4. Her ministries

> As each one has received a special gift, employ it
> in serving one another as good stewards of the
> manifold grace of God.
> ### 1 Peter 4:10

- See that she knows what her ministries are biblically: you, the children, the home, the church body, those outside the faith, and the proportion of time to give to each.
- See that she does not overextend herself.
- Provide her with encouragement in discovering or exercising her spiritual gift(s).

5. Her physical well-being

> So husbands ought also to love their own wives
> as their own bodies. He who loves his own wife
> loves himself; for no one ever hated his own

> flesh, but nourishes and cherishes it, just as
> Christ also does the church.
> **Ephesians 5:28-29**

- See that you show concern for and provide care for any medical issues.
- See that you encourage her and hold her accountable toward proper care of herself: eating, resting, safety, and exercise.

Know When To Act

I think it has been well established that a good leader is not quick to correct. On the other hand, a husband will have times when he *should* speak up (Proverbs 25:11; 27:5). A situation may call for anything from a simple question to a loving rebuke. There may even be times when a husband has to pursue church discipline. If a husband has the right heart (a shepherd's heart and a servant's heart), he will do it at the right time and in the right way. The following are good things to practice *before* you give direction to your wife:

1. Make sure you have adequate information.

> He who gives an answer before he hears, it is folly
> and shame to him.
> **Proverbs 18:13**

- Observe, but be careful not to be presumptuous (thinking you know her heart and mind just by your observation).
- Get information from your wife and any others who can be helpful.
- Obtain biblical insight by studying God's Word and/or seeking godly counsel.

2. Pray for biblical wisdom.

> But if any of you lacks wisdom, let him ask of
> God, who gives to all generously and without
> reproach, and it will be given to him.
> **James 1:5**

- Ask yourself:
  - "Is my input really necessary at this point?"
  - "What is God's perspective on the matter at hand?"
  - "Is this a sin issue or an issue that is causing great difficulty for my wife or family?

3. Think through the proper approach.

Remember, you want to shepherd your wife. What is the most gracious way you can provide her with the opportunity to head in the desired direction on her own initiative? The following questions will help you determine the proper approach. They are placed in a suggested order of progression.

- Have I told my wife what I appreciate about her and what she is doing right?
- Have I made sure she has been given the knowledge or biblical insight that is needed for the change she needs to make?
- Have I given her a chance to apply that knowledge on her own?
- Have I encouraged any progress in the right direction?
- Have I offered any help?
- Have I given her general direction?
- Have I given her specific direction?

When your wife needs specific leadership, you may need to give her a direct instruction or make a definite decision. This should be done in a loving and helpful way. Hopefully, your suggestions will be appreciated, but they may be resented or even resisted. At this point, unless you are asking your wife to sin, *she* is sinning if she refuses to do what you ask.

4. Have the right goals.

> **Whether, then, you eat or drink or whatever you do, do all to the glory of God.**
> **1 Corinthians 10:31**

- Your goals in leading your wife should be:
  - To glorify God
  - To do your wife and others good
  - Not to simply have your way or accomplish your preferences

5.   If at all possible, remember to communicate your reasons and goals (God's glory and the other's good) when you must go against what your wife wants or believes is best (Philippians 2:3-4; Mark 10:32-40).

> **But the goal of our instruction is love from a pure heart and a good conscience and sincere faith.**
> **1 Timothy 1:5**

Leading an Unsaved Wife

Some husbands are married to unbelieving wives. They are still responsible to be faithful in leadership. If a wife professes to believe, but there is doubt as to whether she really is saved or not, a husband should attempt to lead her in the same way a husband should lead a believing wife. In time, her true spiritual condition will become evident. If a husband is married to a wife who readily admits that she is not a believer, he needs to know the answer to the question, "How does a believing husband shepherd an unbelieving wife?"

The most important thing for a husband in this position is to focus on glorifying God no matter what happens. Leading an unsaved wife may prove to be a difficult task, but God has given us some guidance.

> **But to the rest I say, not the Lord, that if any brother has a wife who is an unbeliever, and she consents to live with him, he must not divorce her. And a woman who has an unbelieving husband, and he consents to live with her, let her not send her husband away. For the unbelieving husband is sanctified through his wife, and the unbelieving wife is sanctified through her believing husband; for otherwise your children are unclean, but now they are holy. Yet if the unbelieving one leaves, let him leave; the brother or the sister is not under bondage in such cases, but God has called us to peace. For how do you know, O wife, whether you will save your husband? Or how do you know, O husband, whether you will save your wife?**
> **1 Corinthians 7:12-16**

If you desire to be faithful in leading your unsaved wife:

- *Do not leave her or send her away*, but be willing to live with her and love her (exceptions: unrepentant sexual unfaithfulness or if she wants out of the marriage).

- *Be a godly witness more by your life than by your words.* Seek to be an example of love and obedience toward God. A husband should be careful not to preach at his unsaved wife or force God's Word upon her. Instead, he should share with her only if she is open to hearing about who God is and how to be rightly related to Him.

- *Genuinely love and care for her and have Christ's humble mindset.* Consider her interests and preferences above your own. In my experience, very few unbelieving wives resist coming to the Lord when a husband is living with her in a loving and under-standing way. A husband of an unsaved wife must first of all be sure that he is walking humbly before God and his wife. Many unsaved wives have bailed out of their marriages because their believing husbands were very proud and difficult to live with.

- *When you sin against her, acknowledge it, confess it, ask for her forgive-ness, and then repent* (change).

- *If you are newly saved, allow your unsaved wife a transition time before you try to address sin problems.* First, center on your walk with the Lord and then on her salvation.

- *Do not expect your unbelieving wife to understand her need to honor God with her life or to understand biblical submission.* Since she is an unbeliever, expect her to sin a great deal. Only address major sin that is greatly affecting her or the family. When you must deal with sin, appeal to her conscience and on the basis of what is right in the sight of God and all men. She may or may not understand these things.

- *Remember it is God who saves* (Ephesians 2:1-9). Pray for the Holy Spirit to work and then be patient.

Husbands of unsaved wives often ask questions like, "How can I expect her to submit?" "How can I deal with her sin?" "What do I do if she will not follow?" or "What about matters that pertain to the children and her dealings with them?"

The goal of an exemplary husband who is dwelling with an unbelieving wife should be faithfulness to God's will. A husband cannot *make* his wife submit to Christ, submit to him, or even stay in the relationship. If you have an unsaved wife, you must *not* have the goal of having a saved wife or the goal of a smooth marriage. If your unbelieving wife wants out of the marriage, you should let her go peacefully, because you are called to peace and not war (1 Corinthians 7:15). When a husband has done all he can to love his unbelieving wife, but she still wants to leave, God can give you all the wisdom and grace you need to please Him in this trial. If your unbelieving wife does leave you, it will be an enormous comfort to know that you have glorified God by your faithfulness.

Know How To Make God-Honoring Decisions

A leader will only be as good as his decision-making practices. Because we make hundreds of decisions a day, we must know how to make them in a way that pleases God. The most common mistakes, by far, in decision-making are subjectivity (determining truth by one's own ideas, feelings, or experience) and mysticism (believing that God communicates His will subjectively). J.I. Packer once wrote, "wrong ideas about God's guidance lead to wrong conclusions about what to do." We cannot depend on anything subjective as being from God (see Chapter 5 for decision making principles). In His book, *Decision-Making and the Will of God*, Gary Friesen warns against making important decisions based on our feelings or impressions:

> For impressions could be produced by any number of sources: God, Satan, an angel, a demon, human emotion (such as fear and ecstacy), hormonal imbalance, insomnia, medication, or an upset stomach... Impres-sions are real; believers experience them. But impressions are not authoritative (Multnomah Press: Portland, OR).

Though it is sometimes easier to make decisions subjectively or mystically, God has given us a different and better way to make decisions: by the serious and constant consideration of God's Word (Psalm 1; 19:7; 2 Peter 1:19).

The more you know the Scriptures, the more direction you will have in your life (Psalm 119). There are more than enough principles in the Bible to lead the way. The Bible speaks about some things very *directly* (i.e., direct commands). In this sense it is a specific road map. On other issues, however, the Bible speaks *indirectly* and acts more as a compass, giving you a general direction to follow (i.e., supported principles). John Charles Ryle, the Bishop of Liverpool in 1880, summed up decision-making well when he wrote:

> The Bible must be our standard. Whenever we are confronted with a question about Christian practice, we must apply the teaching of the Bible. Sometimes the Bible will deal with it directly, and we must go by its direct teaching. Often the Bible will not deal with it directly, and then we must look for general *principles* to guide us. It does not matter what other people think. Their behavior is not a standard for us. But the Bible is a standard for us, and it is by the Bible that we must live (emphasis his).

Once you have investigated and applied any direct commands and indirect principles concerning a decision, you may see that the situation falls in the realm of *purposeful freedom*. If you have followed the map and the compass as far as it can take you, you may still have a green light in a certain direction. To a degree, you can then choose however you want to choose, and then trust in the sovereignty of God. While you may have a measure of freedom in your choice, you must always consider the good of others and the need to be a good witness for Christ (1 Corinthians 8:9). This consideration is what I mean by *purposeful* freedom. Your freedom can still be restricted somewhat by certain issues. Here are some questions you can ask yourself when you think you are dealing with an area of freedom:

- Will this choice be an opportunity for my sinful flesh to seek fulfillment? (Romans 13:14; Galatians 5:13; 1 Peter 2:16)
- Will this choice be inconsiderate (self-serving) of someone else? (Philippians 2:3-4)
- Will this choice cause someone else to fall into temptation? (1 Corinthians 8:9-13)

- Will this lead me toward enslavement or addiction? (1 Corinthians 6:12)
- Does this glorify God in every way? (1 Corinthians 10:31)

As you face a leadership decision, be sure to consult your wife in your initial data gathering process. Occasionally, you may go through the whole biblical decision-making process as best you can and still have some reservations due to a lack of information or the desire to get more counsel. In Romans, Paul discourages us from taking any action when we cannot act in full faith. He says, "Whatever is not from faith is sin" (Romans 14:23). Just be sure that you don't use this principle as an excuse to do *nothing*.

Know When To Stand Strong

A good leader will not vacillate on the basis of popular opinion. Once you believe that you have come to a biblical decision, you must not waver just because others don't like it. Strongly evaluate your wife's input and concerns, but also remember, you will answer to God for how you lead. The more carefully you have made a decision the more confident you will be. A husband should not refuse to hear and consider new information (Proverbs 18:1-2), but he must always fear God rather than man. You must ask yourself what Paul asked himself:

> For am I now seeking the favor of men, or of God? Or am I striving to please men? If I were still trying to please men, I would not be a bond-servant of Christ.
>
> **Galatians 1:10**

It is hard to follow someone who doesn't seem to know what he is doing. If you are not careful and biblical about your decision-making, you will most likely change direction or change your decisions often. This instability does not give your wife confidence in your ability to lead. Granted, she still must follow and trust God's sovereignty, but in love you should make it as easy and enjoyable as possible for her to follow you.

Now It's Time To Practice

With a good understanding of the kind of leader God wants us to be and some practical ways to get the job done, the only thing left is for us to be doing it! We need to know our direction and goals. We need to know the areas in which to oversee and lead. We need to know how to make biblical decisions. Then, depending on God, we can work at becoming more and more like our faithful Shepherd-leader and Servant-leader, Jesus Christ. For the glory of God and the furtherance of His kingdom, we need to be exemplary in our leadership. Is your leadership in place and becoming more and more like Christ's?

Chapter Six
BIBLICAL DECISION-MAKING

A leader will only be as good as his decision-making practices. Because we make hundreds of decisions a day, we must know how to make them in a way that pleases God. Before we can begin to understand how God's will and our choices fit together, we must clearly and biblically define the terms and discuss some key presuppositions that apply to the topic of decision-making.

Defining the Terms

Some of these terms may be different from what you have heard or have always thought. Some of them may not have entered your mind at all. Carefully read through these terms and the Scriptures that support them so we can begin on common ground.

God's Will is divided into two aspects: The Decretive will of God and the Preceptive will of God. Confusion concerning these two, or not acknowledging both aspects and their differences, has led many a Christian astray in their decision-making practices.

> **God's Decretive Will** is everything that God ordains (decides, plans) to happen. God's decreed will is a very detailed and predetermined plan (Psalm 119:16; Acts 2:23). This is God's secret plan for the most part. Though many people try to ascertain God's decretive will ahead of time, we can only know it for sure *after* it happens. For instance, a husband can know with absolute certainty that God decreed for him to marry his wife because the marriage ceremony actually took place. On occasion, God has chosen to reveal His decretive will (ahead of time) through Old Testament or early Church prophets. These instances are recorded in the Bible as *future prophecy*.

> Remember the former things long past, for I am
> God and there is no other; I am God, and there
> is no one like Me, declaring the end from the
> beginning, and from ancient times things which
> have not been done, saying, "My purpose will be
> established, and I will accomplish all My good
> pleasure."
>
> **Isaiah 46:9-10**

God's Preceptive (The Revealed) Will is God's moral, lawful, and directional will that He sets forth *in the Bible* for us to follow. It is *revealed* through direct command and through precept (biblically-derived principles). We can know God's preceptive will *ahead of time* because it has already been revealed to us in the Bible. For instance, you can know that you are in the will of God when you choose a legal job over an illegal one, because God tells us in His Word to obey the governing authorities (Romans 13:1-2). The more we know God's revealed will and obey it, the more we will be within the will of God as a man (Psalm 119:1-4).

Sovereignty is the sum total of the attributes of God that allow Him to rule over and control all things with absolute perfection (authority, power, knowledge, wisdom, righteousness). Because God is completely sovereign, His decretive will is *always* accomplished and anything that is not within His plan *does not* happen. This means that whatever actually happens is part of His decreed will. Even sin is a part of His plan, in that He plans to allow it. We know that God is not the author of sin (James 1:3) but He perfectly and wisely chooses to *withhold His restraining influence over sinful hearts* in situations when He can use it to accomplish His good and perfect purposes. For those who love God, He is always working His best in their lives (Romans 8:28). We are still held responsible for our sinful choices, however, because they are *our own* sinful choices from our own sinful hearts. Knowing that all the events in our lives and all the choices we make fall under the sovereignty of God can be very reassuring as long as you trust that He is an all-wise and good God who is afflicted when we are afflicted (Isaiah 63:9) and who is willing to assist us in our trouble (Genesis 50:20; Isaiah 41:10; Isaiah 46:11; Proverbs 21:1; 20:24).

The Providence of God is the secret and purposeful working out of God's decreed will by God, through the orchestrating of all events and people. God is so powerful and so complex that He can cause or prevent whatever His perfect plan prescribes for every person any given day, hour and minute. This means that whatever God allows in your life as a man is for a specific purpose (Ephesians 1:11).

Mysticism is subjectivity applied to the spiritual realm. It believes that spiritual reality and truth are verifiable by inward feelings, judgment, and experience. It also believes that one has a special receiving line or *method of communication* coming from God even though that method is not substantiated by God's Word. For example, a person who believes that God wants him to join a par- ticular church because he felt warm and tingly inside when he thought of it is an example of a mystical person. This person believes that God is communicating with him in a "special" way. R. B. Kuiper refers to this as "Presumptuous Mysticism" and says, "It is the essence of mysticism to separate the operation of the Holy Spirit from God's objective word." He goes on further, "To claim special revelations of God's will by the Holy Spirit apart from the Scriptures sounds pious, but in reality it is wicked presumption which lays him who makes the claim wide open to deception by Satan."

The Christian should reject mystical experiences, because God has chosen to relate to man by means of man's mind, not through his emotions. The Word, which must be understood, is the ultimate [test] of truth and God's will. Subjective experience is not an adequate basis by which to judge the truth of anything. And likewise, the idea of a mystical being a revelation from God, must also be rejected. (Arthur L. Johnson, *Faith Misguided, Exposing the Dangers of Mysticism.* Chicago, IL: Moody Press, 1988, p. 41). Man of God, guard against the temptation to devise a mystical means of communication with God (Colossians 2:8-9). We can have a very personal God who is intimately involved in our lives and leading us each day without mysticism! We will discuss this matter in more detail later in the chapter.

Wisdom is biblical knowledge practically applied to a holy end. Wisdom usually concerns a collection of truths, rather than a single fact. It helps us to discern God's perspective of all ideas, decisions and practices. God promises to give us the wisdom we need to *understand and apply His truth* to our decisions, but we must earnestly pray in faith and we must search His Word. This is how we know what to do. You should not ask God to mystically reveal to you what he wants you to do (Psalm 19:7; James 1:5; 3:13-18).

Biblical Decision-Making Presuppositions

You must begin the biblical decision-making process with some crucial presuppositions. A presupposition is what you assume to be true and therefore act upon. The following are biblical truths that you must be convinced of before you will make decisions biblically. Carefully consider these presuppositions and think about your own assumptions about decision-making before you use the following.

1. *We do not need to know God's decreed will and how He is providentially bringing it about before we make a decision.* **We are *never* told to *search for* or to *try and ascertain* God's decreed (circumstantial) will or to *interpret* God's providence for decision-making.** These are secret things, belonging only to God. Instead, we must trust that He is in control and that He is good. God wants you to determine His will in *another* way. There is only one way for us to know the mind of God— by what He has revealed in His Word. This truth means that you do not have to figure out whether or not God has decreed for you to move before you can make the right decision about moving (Isaiah 55:8-9).

    > ✗ The secret things belong to the Lord our God, but
    > the things revealed belong to us and to our sons
    > forever, that we may observe all the words of this
    > law.
    > **Deuteronomy 29:29**

2. *The Holy Spirit's role is to convict, teach, encourage and conform us— all through the vehicle of the Word of God.* **We are *never* given any promise or instruction that He will *subjectively reveal* to us God's decreed (circumstantial) will ahead of time.** This truth means that a man should not expect some mystical direction from God to determine whether or not he should talk to his wife about an issue. He needs to refer to biblical principles to make his decision and obey.

> But the Helper, the Holy Spirit, whom the Father will send in My name, He will teach you all things, and bring to your remembrance all that I said to you. . . . And He, when He comes, will convict the world concerning sin and righteousness and judgment.
>
> **John 14:26; 16:8**

3. *God only guides or leads his people today: (1) by providence (we know it after the fact) and (2) by Scripture (we can know it before we act).* This truth means that you can stop trying to decipher signs and feelings.

> Your counsel will guide me, and afterward receive me to glory.
>
> **Psalm 73:24**

> Many plans are in a man's heart, but the counsel of the Lord will stand.
>
> **Proverbs 19:21**

4. *God is a gracious God who has provided everything we need to do what He wants us to do.* The Bible is sufficient to guide us in all matters of eternal life and godliness (sanctification) including decision-making. Therefore, **it offers enough insight for us to make *every* decision a God-honoring one.** This truth means that God is not hiding His will from you and that you *can* know it.

> Your word is a lamp to my feet and a light to my path.
>
> **Psalm 119:105**

> Seeing that his divine power has granted to us everything pertaining to life and godliness, through the true knowledge of Him who called us by His own glory and excellence.
>
> **2 Peter 1:3**

5. *God holds us fully responsible to search out and follow His preceptive will (God's written Word) in all of life.* This truth means that **we as men we will be held responsible for making all our decisions by weighing the objective (factual, outside ourselves) Word of God.**

    > **This book of the law shall not depart from your mouth, but you shall meditate on it day and night, so that you may be careful to do according to all that is written in it; for then you will make your way prosperous, and then you will have success.**
    > **Joshua 1:8**

6. *If we make a decision based on biblical commands and principles alone we can fully trust that* ***we are pleasing God*** *in our decision and fully trust that* ***He will providentially (by circumstances out of our control) change our choice if it is not within His decreed will.*** This truth means that you don't have to second-guess yourself anymore.

    > **I have chosen the faithful way; I have placed Your ordinances before me.**
    > **Psalm 119:30**

    > **The mind of man plans his way, but the Lord directs his steps.**
    > **Proverbs 16:9**

7. *To* ***rightly interpret*** *and apply the Word of God we must use a prayerful, literal, historical, contextual, and grammatical method of studying it.* This truth means that if your Bible has been on the shelf, it's time to dust it off! If you read your Bible, but you don't really study it and meditate on it, it's time to get busy! Two helpful books on how to study the Bible are: *How to Interpret the Bible*, by Richard Mayhue (Christian Focus Publications) and *How to Get the Most from Your Bible*, by John F. MacArthur (Word Publications).

    > **Be diligent to present yourself approved to God as a workman who does not need to be ashamed, accurately handling the word of truth.**
    > **2 Timothy 2:15**

> **But know this first of all, that no prophecy of Scripture is a matter of one's own interpretation.**
> **2 Peter 1:20**

8. *No one is ever outside of God's decreed plan.* **We cannot miss the decreed will of God** because God is sovereign. This truth means that you can stop regretting that you didn't choose the other job once you have confessed any *wrong* way you may have decided. All is not lost. God is going to work it all together for good, for everyone.

> **And we know that for those who love God all things work together for good, for those who are called according to His purpose.**
> **Romans 8:28**

Subjectivity and Decision-Making

The most common mistakes, by far, in decision-making are subjectivity (determining truth by one's own ideas, feelings, or experience) and mysticism (believing that God communicates His will subjectively). J.I. Packer once wrote, "Wrong ideas about God's guidance lead to wrong conclusions about what to do." We cannot depend on anything subjective as being from God. In His book, *Decision-Making and the Will of God,* Gary Friesen warns against making important decisions based on our feelings or impressions:

> For impressions could be produced by any number of sources: God, Satan, an angel, a demon, human emotion (such as fear and ecstasy), hormonal imbalance, insomnia, medication, or an upset stomach...Impressions are real; believers experience them. But impressions are not authoritative (Multnomah Press: Portland, OR).

Some Christians make poor decisions because they do not understand that God no longer communicates His will outside the pages of Scripture. They read the Old Testament and assume that God guides the average believer today in much the same way that He guided His people before His written Word was in existence.

Some people also believe that God will individually speak to them because He spoke individually to His special prophets and Apostles. From the New Testament, however, we understand that God communicated to these individuals in special ways, *in order* to provide us with the all-sufficient and eternal Word of God (2 Peter 1:21, 1 Thessalonians 2:13).

Once the Word of God was complete there was no more need for such individual communication. In fact, once the Apostles were verified as the final authentic spokesmen for God, all individual communications from God ceased (2 Peter 2:19; Hebrews 1:1-2). Read what the Westminster Confession of Faith states:

> The whole counsel of God concerning all things necessary for his own glory, man's salvation, faith *and life*, is either expressly set down in Scripture, or by good and necessary consequences may be deduced from Scripture: unto which nothing at any time is to be added, whether by new revelations of the Spirit, or traditions of men. (Emphasis mine, *The Westminster Standards, Confession of Faith*, Ch. I, VI; Philadelphia, Penn., The Great Commission Publications, 1989)

Just because God no longer communicates with us *individually*, however, does not mean that He does not communicate to us *personally* today. His written Word to us is very *personal communication* (John 16:13-15). The Holy Spirit's job is to make it even more *personal* (1 Corinthians 2:12-13). Some will strongly argue that God has individually spoken to them in one way or another, but there is no way for them to verify or trust the source of their experience, not even for themselves. Only God knows the true source of whatever they believe they have received. Just because they are *fully convinced* does not mean that they see things as they really are. Many deluded individuals have heard voices or become fully convinced of things that are clearly not true. We must measure our experiences by the objective word of God and not vice versa (e.g., Deuteronomy 13:1-4).

Some people make decisions subjectively because this is the norm for our society. Many people are feelings oriented. Some regularly use the term "feel" in place of "believe" or "think" (e.g., "How do you 'feel' about...?"). One of the reasons our society has become subjective is because it has an aversion to absolutes. For a person who does not want to recognize the Bible as the authoritative Word of God, any way of making decisions would be a better one than making decisions based on the Bible. Also, man's flesh has a natural bent towards doing things the easy way. Certainly it is easier to live life by feelings and/or signs, rather than by the hard work of engaging the mind in study. Naturally, the undisciplined and lazy person will not want to give the time or mental effort it takes to make a biblical decision. God's way of doing things is rarely the easy way, but His way always results in the greatest reward (Galatians 6:9).

K. B. Kuiper in his online article, *Pitfalls in finding God's Will for Your Life* addresses the kind of mysticism and subjectivity that is so prevalent among Christians today. Here is a quoted worth contemplating.

> This type of mysticism frequently expresses itself in prayers that in the site of God must be abominations. Instead of praying that the Holy Spirit may make the divine will in a given matter clear from Scripture, one prays only to be led to know God's will and puts forth no effort to discover it from His word. That amounts to tempting God as much as if a drunkard were to enter a saloon with the prayer on his lips: "Lead me not into temptation." And how dreadfully easy it becomes for such a one to convince himself that whatever he feels like doing after prayer for guidance cannot possibly be wrong.

Making decisions by subjective means will usually result in disappointment or even disaster. We must be sure that our way of deciding what to do is not based on former ways that God used to deal with His people (Hebrews 1:1-2), on our imaginations (Ezekiel 13:2-3, 7), on something that *seems* miraculous (Deuteronomy 13:1-4), or on our own selfish desires (Proverbs 14:12; 18:1-2).

> Son of man, prophesy against the prophets of
> Israel who prophesy, and say to those who proph-
> esy from their own inspiration, 'Listen to the word
> of the Lord!' Thus says the Lord God, 'Woe to the
> foolish prophets who are following their own
> spirit and have seen nothing. . . . Did you not see
> a false vision, and speak a lying divination when
> you said, "The Lord declares," but it is not I who
> have spoken?'
>
> Ezekiel 13:2-3, 7

Subjective means to avoid or be cautious of:

1. Misusing the Bible: This method involves trying to obtain biblical direction by the *open-the-Bible-and-point* method or by looking for a message from God in your daily Bible reading that will mystically tell you what He wants you to do. Both of these methods take God's Word out of its context. Instead we need to study God's Word rightly to understand the *one thing* that He meant and apply that truth to our lives. Hopefully this is not the way you decided to marry your spouse.

2. Personal advice: This is using what others think for direction when it is not founded upon biblical principles but rather on opinion and experience alone. Advice from those who are godly enough to tell you what God does and doesn't say about the matter can be very valuable, how ever. Either way, never use personal advice *alone* to make your decisions. A man might find himself changing jobs or churches every few months by always being swayed by others' opinion and experience (Psalm 1:1-2; Proverbs 14:12; 25:19; Isaiah 55:8-9).61

3. Circumstances/results: This is assuming that you can under-stand what God wants you to do by reading or interpreting certain circumstances or results. Many grave mistakes have been made based on what the circumstances "seemed to say." There was once a man who experienced great confusion from reading the circumstances in order to deter- mine if he should become a missionary. At one point the circumstances began to say, "You've made a mistake." He was turned down by three mission boards. He was even more confused when the people he was finally able to minister to never responded to his missionary efforts. The Bible teaches us that sometimes God's

path is not easy. Also God often sent prophets to people that did not listen. There is no way to be certain what circumstances or results mean (Numbers 20:8-12; Joshua 9; Proverbs 13:16).

4. <u>Setting up conditions</u>: This is imposing a condition on God for direction. If the condition comes true then one considers that God has communicated His answer. This mystical means of decision-making is similar to reading circumstances, only with a presumptuous (assuming on or testing God) twist. For lack of trust in God's faithfulness to do what He said He would do, Gideon of the Bible did this very thing by laying out a wool fleece for God to give him a sign on (Judges 6:36-40). Because God was merciful to Gideon at a time when His written Word was not complete, this does not mean that we can assume that it is okay to put God to the test. A man who uses this method might tell God, "If you want me to go back to school, have someone call me in the next hour and tell me it is a good idea." He might even use spiritual lingo like, "Lord, I'm going to trust you for..." (Matthew 4:5; Psalm 19:13).

5. <u>Opened and closed doors:</u> This is using opportunities or the loss of an opportunity as a message from God about what you should do. In the Bible, opened and closed doors are *never* used in this way. In fact, Paul did not take one door that was opened to him even though it was acceptable (not sinful) to the Lord (2 Corinthians 2:12-13). It is usually spoken of in Scripture concerning an opportunity to share the gospel, *after* the fact—*not* as a means of determining God's direction. Assuming that an opened door is in itself the very direction of God can cause a man to make very bad decisions and even a husband to neglect his family (Acts 14:27; 1 Corinthians 16:9).

6. <u>Ideas, inner feelings, desires and impressions:</u> This is interpreting some- thing from *within* as the "voice" of God. Contrary to popular opinion, just because an idea, feeling, desire, etc. seems "good," this does not mean it is of God. Any one of these things from within could be from self or the Evil One. Garry Friesen writes in his book, *Decision Making and the Will of God:*

> For impressions could be produced by any number of sources: God, Satan, an angel, a demon, human emotions (such as fear or ecstasy), hormonal imbalance, insomnia, medication,

or an upset stomach. ...Impressions are real; believers experience them. But impressions are *not authoritative*. (Emphasis Friesen's, Multnomah Press, Portland Oregon, 1980, pp. 130-131)

Some people believe that if they love the Lord and strongly desire something that seems good, that desire is from God. A verse that is often taken out of context is Psalm 37:4:

Delight yourself in the Lord; and He will give you the desires of your heart.

A person cannot assume that just because they love God, *every* desire they have is from Him. What this verse *does* mean is the more you delight in God, the more you will desire the right kinds of things. Feelings can be attributed to our thinking, our physical condition or our spiritual state, but not as a message from God.

Interpreting inner "signs" as God's direction could lead a man to commit sin. A husband might even divorce his wife without biblical grounds because "God communicated that it was okay" (2 Samuel 7:1-7; Matthew 16:4; 16:21-23).

7. An audible voice: This is hearing a voice that is not coming from a person who is speaking to you and believing it to be the audible voice of God. *This is very dangerous*. If you are hearing voices, it is either *satanic* in origin (only possible for unbelievers) or a *personal delusion* stemming from sleep loss, a mind that knows no bounds or from living in gross sin. Even if what you "hear" seems good and right you must not assume that it is from God or that it should be acted upon. We know that God does not intend to add *anything* to His Word (Hebrews 1:1-2; 2 Peter 1:17-21). 63

8. Misusing prayer: This is believing that you can receive some sort of message from God through prayer. This is nothing more than putting stock in ideas/inner feelings/desires/ impressions that you receive while you are praying. The purpose of prayer is *not* to **receive** anything (but strength) from God but to **give** confessions, praises, thanksgiving, and petitions, to **align** our thinking with God's thinking, and to **express** our dependence and trust. Men, we must be sure that we are not looking for a sign or a feeling from God

when we pray! When Jesus taught the disciples to pray he gave a model prayer which did not include receiving any messages from God (Luke 11:2-4). (For verses showing the fallacy of interpreting ideas, inner feelings, or desires as direction from God, see #6.)

9. <u>Inner peace:</u> This is interpreting a sense of peace or an unrest in your soul as direction from God. This is also a feeling. We are commanded to be at peace with God (salvation). We are also commanded to be at peace in our mind (free from anxiety). We are even commanded to be at peace with one another (as much as depends on us). If we are truly not at peace, we are in sin. If someone is using the phrase "I don't have peace about it" to mean they have a gut feeling that they shouldn't do something or to mean that God is letting them know that they shouldn't do something—this is subjective and totally unreliable. If they mean, "I feel troubled about making that choice because I am thinking about certain things that concern me" or "because I don't have enough information to make a wise (or holy) decision," this is a matter of wisdom and discernment which involves factual data, God's wisdom, and the thinking process—*not just feelings.*

It would be better to say, "I can't be sure that this is a wise (or holy) decision yet." This is exactly the case with Paul in 2 Corinthians 2:13. He had no "rest for his spirit" because he did not *think* it was wise to go to Troas without Titus. Paul was not saying that his unrest was a message from God. Nine times out of ten a person is "not at peace" about a decision because of something they are thinking and they mistakenly attribute their feelings to a mystical message from God. If their feeling is not from their thinking, it could be from any number of physical or personal reasons (desires). Whether or not a person has inner peace is never used for decision-making in the Bible. When you are uneasy about a decision, determine what you are thinking about the facts that are involved or your own desires. Brother, sometimes what you feel worst about is the most right thing to do (Romans 5:1; 12:18; Philippians 4:6-9; Colossians 3:14-15).

There are varying views about the definitions, presuppositions, and methods we have discussed. Many people are not sure what they believe, which causes them to move in and out of different views. God has given us a far better way to make decisions than by these subjective means. Before a person will turn to the biblical way of making decisions, they must see the fallacy of these subjective decision-making methods. They must not trust their own judgment.

> **There is a way which seems right to a man, but**
> **its end is the way of death.**
> **Proverbs 16:25**

Every man of God must acknowledge that Scripture does not support these methods as means of determining God's will. In his book, *Reckless Faith,* John MacArthur writes:

> [Very] ... significant ... is the fact the *Scripture never commands us to tune into any inner voice.* We are commanded to study and meditate on Scripture (Joshua 1:8; Psalm 1:1-2). We're instructed to cultivate wisdom and discernment (Proverbs 4:5-8). We're told to walk wisely and make the most of our time (Ephesians 5:15-16). We're ordered to be obedient to God's commands (Deuteronomy 28:1-2; John 15:14). But we are never encouraged to listen for inner promptings. (Emphasis MacArthur's, p. 192, Crossway Books, Wheaton, Ill., 1994)

The Word of God presents and provides a more sure way of living in the will of God. It lifts it self above any subjective means that was used in the days of long ago.

> **We ourselves heard this very voice borne form**
> **heaven, for we were with him on the holy moun-**
> **tain.** *And we have something more sure*, **the pro-**
> **phetic word, to which you will do well to pay**
> **attention as to a lamp shining in a dark place,**
> **until the day dawns and the morning star rises in**
> **your hearts, knowing this first of all that no**
> **prophesy of scripture comes from someone's own**
> **interpretation.**
> **2 Peter 1:18-20**

Making God Honoring Decisions

Though it is sometimes easier to make decisions selfishly, subjectively or mystically, God has given us a different and better way: by the serious and specific consideration of God's Word (Psalm 1; 19:7; 2 The more you know the Scriptures, the more direction you will have in your life (Psalm 119). There are *more* than enough principles in the Bible to lead the way. In this section we will explain the dynamics of biblical decision-making and the diagram tool that follows. You may want to follow the chart as you read.

The Bible speaks about some things very *directly* (i.e., direct commands). In this sense it is a specific road map. On other issues, however, the Bible speaks *indirectly* and acts more as a compass, giving you a general direction to follow (i.e., supported principles). John Charles Ryle, the Bishop of Liverpool in 1880, summed up decision-making well when he wrote:

> The Bible must be our standard. Whenever we are confronted with a question about Christian practice, we must apply the teaching of the Bible. Sometimes the Bible will deal with it directly, and we must go by its direct teaching. Often the Bible will not deal with it directly, and then we must look for general *principles* to guide us. It does not matter what other people think. Their behavior is not a standard for us. But the Bible is a standard for us, and it is by the Bible that we must live (emphasis his).

Once you have investigated and applied any direct commands and indirect principles concerning a decision, you may see that the situation falls in the realm of *purposeful freedom*. If you have followed the map and the compass as far as it can take you, you may still have a green light in a certain direction. To a degree, you can then choose however you want to choose, and then trust in the sovereignty of God. While you may have a measure of freedom in your choice, you must always consider the good of others and the need to be a good witness for Christ (1 Corinthians 8:9). This consideration is what I mean by *purposeful* freedom. Your freedom can still be restricted somewhat by certain issues. Here are some questions you can ask yourself when you think you are dealing with an area of freedom:

- Will this choice be an opportunity for my sinful flesh to seek fulfillment? (Romans 13:14; Galatians 5:13; 1 Peter 2:16)
- Will this choice be inconsiderate (self-serving) of someone else? (Philippians 2:3-4)
- Will this choice cause someone else to fall into temptation? (1 Corinthians 8:9-13)
- Will this lead me toward enslavement or addiction? (1 Corinthians 6:12)
- Does this glorify God in every way? (1 Corinthians 10:31)

As you face a significant leadership decision, be sure to consult others (any one else involved, other godly men/leaders and of course your wife if you have one) in your initial data gathering process. Occasionally, you may go through the whole biblical decision-making process as best you can and still have some reservations due to a lack of information or the desire to get more counsel. In Romans, Paul discourages us from taking any action when we cannot act in full faith. He says, "Whatever is not from faith is sin" (Romans 14:23). Just be sure that you don't use this principle as an excuse to do *nothing*!

Biblical Decision-Making
Diagram Tool

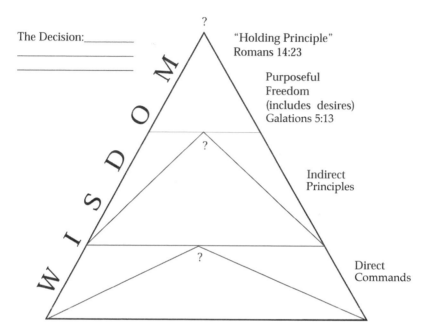

The Decision:_____
_____
_____

? (top)

"Holding Principle"
Romans 14:23

Purposeful
Freedom
(includes desires)
Galations 5:13

Indirect
Principles

Direct
Commands

WISDOM

Attitude: Prayerfully humbly, to please Christ

Any Factual Data
(Proverbs 18:13):_____
_____
_____
_____
_____

Practice, Pray and Trust

Trusting God's way of decision making and in God's sovereignty is very freeing! The "real man" does not have to worry whether or not he is making the right decision or second guess himself after the decision is made. He can trust that a good God will cause "all things to work together for good" (Romans 8:28) or providentially re-direct his steps if an honest effort is made to honor scriptural principles along his way. So move forward with God's Word in mind and TRUST!

Discovering Problem Patterns

Name _____

Date _____

Directions: For one week carefully list all events, situations or activities (good or bad) that resulted in _____ .
Circle those that occur three or more times.

	Sunday	Monday	Tuesday	Wednesday	Thursday	Friday	Saturday
Morning							
Afternoon							
Evening							

(Used by permission from Zondervan Publishing House (Grant ID:), out of The Christian Counselor's Manual by Jay Adams pg. 280. Grand Rapids, Michigan, 1973.)

Appendicies

Appendix I
AN ENEMY OF BIBLICAL MANHOOD
Lust

One of the most destructive sins to the single man, the husband and the family is that of sexual lust. This sin opens the door to all kinds of degradation, but at the very least it will warp your masculinity, leadership and decision-making in significant ways. In a society that is obsessed with sex, it can be very difficult to gain victory over the sin of lust and the many forms of sexual sin to which it leads. Based on the counseling I have done in the church, I would say that many men find it difficult to remain pure in this area. From the media we are taught that lust is acceptable and normal. This portrayal is very different from how God views lust. Man of God, you must conquer sexual lust before you can grow and be more like Christ.

It can be difficult to see this sin as clearly as God does. A great number of men are involved in sexual sin in one way or another regularly. It doesn't take long to see it take its toll in a man's life and in his relationships. This sin *can* and *will* destroy a man's life and his marriage relationship as no other. Let me emphasize my point by repeating the previous sentence. This sin can and will destroy a man's life and his marriage relationship as no other. Men who would never physically hurt their wives will deeply hurt them within through their use of pornography and through extra-marital affairs.

Because the flesh loves the pleasure of sexual sin so much, many men don't really want to give up their lust. They may hate the guilt and the consequences but not really hate the sin. When one becomes regularly involved with lust and what follows, it can seem impossible to stop. The good news is, however, that all things are possible with God! A person who struggles with lust and other sexual sin, *can* have victory (I Corinthians 6:9-11). Even if you have allowed yourself to become entangled with this sin, you *can* learn new habits and learn to view the sexual area in a wholesome way, if you really want to please God. It will take work to apply God's principles, but perseverance will enable you to overcome your sinful habit. There is great hope, men. The question is, Are you ready to do what God says?

Definition

Most men are familiar with lust, but they may not fully understand what it is and where it comes from. All sexual sin begins with the sin of lust. We need to know what it really is so that we can take full responsibility for it.

The word "lust": The major Greek word for lust is *epithumia*. This word simply means *to have a strong desire that is focused on satisfaction or attaining what is desired.* This Greek word can be used in a good sense. In the Greek septuigent it is used in reference to the "desire of the righteous" (Proverbs 10:24). Jesus "earnestly desired" to eat the Passover with His disciples before He died (Luke 22:15). Paul had a "great desire" to see the Thessalonians (1 Thessalonians 2:17). God even gave instruction to the church concerning the man who "desires" the office of overseer (1 Timothy 3:1). The Bible also uses this word in a bad sense, however. When the word is used negatively, it is usually termed "evil desire" or "lust".

The lust of the flesh is a sinful desire and is quite different from a righteous desire. The desire of the flesh (our unredeemed humanness) is evil of every kind. Lust is nothing more than evil desire looking for fulfillment. It is only looking for *self*-satisfaction. The lust of the flesh can involve any of the bodily appetites and members, but the eyes are usually the initial agent for men. We are commanded not to have "lustful passion, like the Gentiles who do not know God" (1 Thessalonians 4:5). We are also told to "flee youthful lusts and pursue righteousness" (2 Timothy 2:22). Lust is welcoming and continuing in the evil desires of the flesh, rather than resisting them and fleeing from them by turning to God and what is right.

> For the grace of God has appeared, bringing salvation to all men, instructing us to deny ungodliness and worldly desires and to live sensibly, righteously and godly in the present age.
> Titus 2:11-12

Lustful thinking is a grave sin in God's sight, but, if it is toler-ated, it is only the beginning of our lust. Unless our inward thoughts are disciplined, they *will* progress to more outward sin. Sexual lust is usually not satisfied until physical sexual sin achieves selfish fulfillment. Even though it may take days of mental epi-sodes before lust requires complete fulfillment, the flesh does not give up until it is either satisfied or mortified (put to death by say-ing "no" to it's desires, and by putting on righteousness) (Romans 8:13; 13:12-14; Colossians 3:5).

If tolerated, lustful thoughts will progress to actions such as:

- Using one's wife for selfish sex.
- Masturbation (usually using pictures, adult movies, telephone sex calls, Internet chat rooms and sex web sites, or "window watching" for arousal and preliminary enjoyment).
- Sex with a woman other than your wife.
- Sex with another man.
- Sex with a child.
- Sex with an animal.

These sins are the outworking of a regularly lustful heart, and they are abominable to God. A person who commits sins such as these has already given himself over to evil desire long before he carries out the deed. So these *deeds* can also be thought of as lust. Furthermore, we can think of mental lust as very similar to the deeds of lust. Both are following evil sexual desires. Both are sex-ual sin. Now we can understand why Christ said:

"You have heard that is was said, 'You shall not commit adultery;' but I say to you that everyone who looks at a woman with lust for her has already committed adultery with her in his heart."
Matthew 5:27-28

Explanation

Before a man can have victory over lust, he must embrace and act upon certain truths. Just understanding what lust is will not be enough to prepare him for the battle that rages within.

> Finally then, brethren, we request and exhort you
> in the Lord Jesus, that as you received from us
> instruction as to how you ought to walk and please
> God (just as you actually do walk), that you excel
> still more. For you know what commandments we
> gave you by the authority of the Lord Jesus. For
> this is the will of God, your sanctification; that is,
> that you abstain from sexual immorality; that each
> of you know how to possess his own vessel in
> sanctification and honor, not in lustful passion,
> like the Gentiles who do not know God; and that
> no man transgress and defraud his brother in the
> matter because the Lord is the avenger in all these
> things, just as we also told you before and sol-
> emnly warned you. For God has not called us for
> the purpose of impurity, but in sanctification. So
> he who rejects this is not rejecting man but the
> God who gives His Holy Spirit to you.
> 1 Thessalonians 4:1-8

1. The man who desires to put off sin must first delight in Christ Himself and apply the gospel each day to his life. It is Christ who has sacrificed himself for us and graciously broken sin's vice-grip on our hearts, who lives in us to give us the power over sin that we need, who has paid for and made provision for forgiveness of all our sins (though we don't deserve it), who wants to be to us the fountain of living waters, who we will see again in heaven and to whom we owe all gratitude and our very lives. At the time of temptation we are to fight the lies of self and Satan with the truth of Jesus Christ and his gospel (Ephesians 1:3-7; Ephesians 2:1-10). The primary evil of lust is that we have forsaken Christ and turned to something else for hope, help, relief and satisfaction.

> For my people have committed two evils: they
> have forsaken me, the fountain of living waters
> and hewed out cisterns for themselves, broken
> cisterns that can hold no water.
> Jeremiah 2:13

2. <u>Lust involves listening to and believing lies</u>. Some examples are:
   - "This is just a small sin. It doesn't matter. It won't hurt anyone."
   - "But I need to."
   - "I deserve some enjoyment."
   - "I can't resist it. I'm only human."
   - "This activity will be so pleasurable."
   - "I'll never be able to change, so why try? I'll never win against this."
   - "No one will know."
   - "I won't keep doing this. This will be the only or the last time. I don't really have a problem."

   But I am afraid that, as the serpent deceived Eve by his craftiness, your minds will be led astray from the simplicity and purity of devotion to Christ.
   2 Corinthians 11:3

3. <u>There really is no small sin.</u> Sin is not small in God's eyes, and it is a lie of Satan that a little sin doesn't matter. Any sin that is tolerated is a serious matter to God because it always leads to more sin. Lust follows a progression of entanglement. It does not become a life-dominating sin overnight, but it will happen, and in a much shorter time than your flesh wants you to believe. Here is a general progression of the sin of lust.

   a) Failure to worship God (Romans 1:21)
   b) An ungrateful heart (Romans 1:21)
   c) Introduction to sexual sin (Proverbs 3:31,32)
   d) Experiencing sexual sin (Proverbs 10:23)
   e) Repeating the experience of sexual sin (Proverbs 26:11)
   f) Developing a routine or a ritual for your sexual sin (Proverbs 6:18)
   g) Domination by your sexual sin (2 Peter 2:14, 18-19 NKV)
   h) God gives you over to your sexual sin (Romans 1:21-24)
   i) All kinds of degradation (Romans 1:28-32)

A little sin is a very dangerous thing. If you believe this fact, you will avoid sin all the more (Proverbs 5: 3, 8-9,22-23; Proverbs 29:6; and James 1:13-16).

4. Satan wants to destroy you. He is your enemy and will certainly make the most of your fleshly desires. You must be alert and wise to his schemes (1 Peter 5:8-9 and Ephesians 6:10-11; 2 Corinthians 2:11).

5. Sin always has a price. There are always consequences to sin. There is a spiritual consequence—sin always darkens the heart and one's judgement and prevents fellowship with God. There is the consequence of guilt and the effects of guilt (depression, fear, and illness). There are also very often physical consequences such as a difficult life, an unwanted pregnancy, sexually transmitted diseases, the destruction of a relationship, financial difficulties, church discipline, and even criminal conviction. Most important, however, there are eternal consequences that God will carry out if there is no repentance (change). For the Christian, this can include turning him over to death, and for the unbeliever, eternal hell. (Proverbs 21:17; Proverbs 22:8; Matthew 18:17-18; Matthew 19:3-9; Romans 13:2-4; 1 Corinthians 5:5 and 1 Corinthians 6:9-10)

6. There is a war raging. Every husband must be aware that there is a spiritual war raging in his own members (body) and going on around him. Within him, the Spirit wars against the flesh and the flesh wars against the Spirit. If a husband does not prepare for the fight, get into the battle and stay alert, he will be taken captive by the flesh. If we are not walking in the Spirit (being mindful of God, His Word and His righteous path), it is as if we are letting the enemy walk right into our camp. When we are not in total pursuit of righteousness, it is as if we are trying to make friends with the enemy. We will then be easy prey, and we will soon join with the enemy in the fight against the Spirit and all that is righteous. There is also a spiritual war raging against good and evil involving God and His angels and Satan and his angels. But Satan is no match for God, or for you if you are a believer who is dependent on God and pursuing righteousness. (Romans 7:21-25; 2 Corinthians 10:3-6; Galatians 5:16-17; Ephesians 6:12-17; and 1 John 4:4)

7. Expect the battle to be more severe when you first begin to fight. If you are serious about having victory over your sin, you must be ready for a difficult fight. The good news is that you can win, and the more you fight the easier the battle becomes. Victory is sure if you do what God says and endure to the end. (Galatians 6:9; 2 Tim 2:3-4; 1Peter 5:6-10; 1 John 5:4; and Jude 24-25)

8. Lust must be nipped in the bud. The only way to win against the flesh is to not give it a chance. The old saying "give him an inch and he takes a mile" is certainly true of our flesh. It is very important to flee temptation from the outset. We must flee from it to the Lord and to what is righteous instead. Sexual thoughts must be forsaken *immediately* and replaced with righteous ones. (Genesis 39:7-12; 1 Corinthians 10:13; and Romans 13:11-14)

9. Radical action must be taken. The flesh must have no opportunity. This basic truth will often mean taking what may seem to other people to be drastic measures. You must starve the flesh to loosen its grip. You may need to cut out television, movies, and even certain routes of travel for awhile. You may need to graciously cut certain people out of your life. You may need to move. You may need to change jobs. You must figure out how you can make no provision for the flesh by not even allowing it a remote opportunity. Christ was clear that we must take radical action against dominating sin. One of the most important ways of making no provision for the flesh is to make yourself accountable to your wife and a godly man (or men) in your church who can help you stand strong. You should definitely seek their counsel about any drastic changes you think are necessary. (Mark 9:42-48; 1 Corinthians 15:33; and Colossians 3:5-11)

10. The opposite of lust is love. Any man who hopes to rid himself of lust must learn to pursue love with fervency. Lust is purely selfish and often involves taking from or using someone else. One of the best things a man can do to rid himself of lust is to look for ways to show real love (giving), especially to his wife. He needs to give generously to others on a regular basis, but especially when temptation comes. A great way to *start* is to

pray for any person who is a temptation for you. Pray for their spiritual condition or that God would teach and bless them. Be sure that you pray for them briefly (in order to turn your selfishness into love) and then move on to other responsibilities and serving. To continue to dwell on them may give you more opportunity to lust after them. (Matthew 22:39; Romans 12:9-13; 13:8-10 and Ephesians 5:1-4)

11. You must walk in the Spirit to avoid the deeds of the flesh. The best way to win against the flesh is to fix your mind on God and His Word. This is walking in the Spirit. You cannot walk by the flesh and walk in the Spirit at the same time. They are diametrically opposed to one another. The more you walk in the Spirit the more you will do the deeds of the Spirit. (Romans 8:6-8; Galatians 5:16-20; Galatians 6:7-8 and James 1:21-22,25)

12. Lust usually involves other kinds of sin. When a person is living in lust he will most likely commit other sins in order to accomplish his lustful sin. Deceit is almost always involved in sexual sin. One may try to manipulate other people into helping him accomplish his sin, or even enter into it with him. Also, when one is confronted with his sin, he will very likely blame-shift and make excuses for it. A person involved in habitual sexual sin will also sin in other ways simply because he is walking in the flesh. (Proverbs 4:19 and James 3:14-16)

13. A dominating sexual sin *cannot* remain a secret. More than likely, you are only kidding yourself by thinking that you can handle this problem on your own. Lust never really is secret. Even when sin seems secret, it's not. God sees it. Secrecy is helping you to sin. Sin loves isolation. As awful as it may seem to come clean by telling someone who can help, it doesn't compare to the alternative of continuing in your sin, which will only lead to more darkness and degradation. If you want to win against sin, you must let others into your life. Read Numbers 32:23; Psalm 51:4; 69:5; 90:8; Proverbs 15:3 and Jeremiah 16:17.

At this point, I would like to make it clear that you *should* let your wife (the one who is supposed to be 'one' with you) know about your basic struggle and how she can help, but do so with *caution*. You should be honest about your struggle, but it is not necessary to give her all the details. She needs enough information to know how to pray for you, what tempts you, and how she can help hold you accountable, but you don't need to tell her every time you are tempted, or even about every time you have a lustful thought. While she can be a part of your accountability, she should not bear the brunt of the accountability that you need. You *must not* in any way give her the impression that your success or failure is dependent on her. Be sure that you convey to her that the Lord, you, and whoever is helping you are working very hard on the situation, and that *she* does not have to. You and your wife may need to sit down with another godly couple if she is having a very difficult time dealing with the situation, becomes bitter, begins policing you, or refuses to help or deal with the situation at all.

Sexual sin by its very nature leads to isolation. A man who is engaged in "secret" sin will distance himself from others. This distance is because of guilt, the fear of being found out, and the desire to keep sinning. A man who wants to continue in sin will not want to be close to righteous people. A lustful person may also not be a very likeable person because he is selfish, proud, and often angry. He may be somewhat isolated for this reason also. Still, if you struggle with sexual lust as a believer, it is of the utmost importance that you make a friend whom you can tell about your sin problem, and who will help you apply God's principles to it. (Proverbs 18:1 and Proverbs 27:17)

14. Lust can be an idol or a refuge. For many, sexual sin is nothing more than the idol of pleasure. They worship the temporary pleasure their sin brings, rather than worshiping God. They are intent on having worldly pleasure and will sin to get it. For others, sexual sin is more of a refuge in times of trouble or when they cannot have what they are worshiping. They turn to sexual pleasure as a bit of relief from their misery. (Jeremiah 13:25; Romans 1:25; Colossians 3:5 and Psalm 62:5-8)

15. There is more to life than sex. When a man's life is dominated by this sin, everything relates to it. It becomes everything to him. Instead, he must repent of this attitude and find other good things to focus on and do. If you are married, sex should only be a small aspect of your marriage and life. If you are not married, you must forsake the idea altogether. Contrary to

what those who are in bondage think, sexual pleasure does not equal happiness—only knowing, walking with, and serving God does. (Psalm 1:1-2; Colossians 3:1-3; and John 15:7-11)

16. Sex can be holy and pure. If you are married and struggle with lust you must begin to think of sex in a new way. You must plan to take a different path of thinking when you are having intimacy with your wife. It should be an opportunity to bring pleasure to your wife. Sex as God intended it is holy and pure and should be enjoyed. If you seek to give instead of to get, you will enjoy this God-given blessing in a totally new way—a pure and holy way.

17. You can bring glory to God and have a useful life for Him by truly forsaking sin and turning to God. When we lust, God fades from view, and when God fades, we will lust even more. Your heart must be set on God. From Kent and Barbara Hughes' *Liberating Ministry From the Success Syndrome*, Tyndale House Publishers, 1987, p. 89):

> Lay this maxim to heart: *When lust takes control, God is unreal to us.* What a world of wisdom there is in this! When we are in the grip of lust, the reality of God fades. The longer King David gazed, the less real God became. Not only was his awareness of God diminished, but in the growing darkness he lost awareness of who David was—his holy call, his frailty, and the sure consequences of sin.
>
> That is what lust does. It has done it millions of times. Lust makes God disappear, at least in the lust-glazed eyes of those involved. Here, fellow servants, we must once again ask some questions: Is God fading from view? Were you once walking closely with him, but now, because of creeping sensuality he seems but a distant phantom? If so, you must take decisive steps to guard your heart. You must terminate the intake of lustful words and images—whether they be gotten from reading,

or the media, or an acquaintance. If you do not, God will fade and you will fall.

Your sin can be forgiven and made powerless in your life. You will no doubt face temptation, but you can lead a new way of life. Read Isaiah 38:17; Psalm 25:4-9, 18; Psalm 51:9; Acts 3:19 and 1 Corinthians 6:9-11.

Examination

The first step to overcoming your sin problem is to admit that you have one. The second thing you must do is to take full responsibility for it. No one else has caused this problem—not God or anyone who has influenced you. Your sinful heart has chosen to take whatever opportunities you were given because your heart (without God) is utterly wicked. You must be brutally honest with yourself in order to begin on the path of righteousness. Answer the following questions honestly:

Search me, O God, and know my heart; try me and know my anxious thoughts; and see if there be any hurtful way in me, and lead me in the everlasting way.

Psalm 139:23-24

TEST

1. Are you regularly worshiping and communing with God?
2. Are you regularly thankful and grateful to God?
3. Are you content with God alone and His spiritual blessings?
4. Are you focused on loving others?
5. How are you regularly serving others?
6. How are you using your gifts in the church?
7. Do you have sexual thoughts?
8. Do you change sexual thoughts immediately?
9. Have you ever entertained a sexual thought for any length of time?
10. Have you repeated entertaining sexual thoughts?
11. Have you exposed yourself to sexually explicit material?
12. Have you committed any sinful sexual deeds?
13. Have you repeated any sinful sexual deeds? How many times?

14. What do you do when you are down or troubled? Where do you go?
15. Do you regularly commit sexual sin (in thought or deed)?
16. Is there a pattern or a ritual to your sexual sin?
17. How often do you think about sexual things and/or sexual satisfaction?
18. How much is your life ordered around your sin?
19. Would you say that you are in bondage to your sexual sin?
20. Do you view sex as self-satisfaction?
21. Is your sin a secret?
22. What are the effects of your sin?
23. In what other ways are you following the flesh?
24. What other interests do you have?

> **And He was saying to them all, "If anyone wishes to come after Me, he must deny himself, and take up his cross daily and follow Me. For whoever wishes to save his life will lose it, but whoever loses his life for My sake, he is the one who will save it."**
> **Luke 9:23-24**

Transformation

Friend, if you are sinning by committing sexual sin (in thought or deed), God says you must repent (Acts 26:20). The question is, are you really willing to repent? Are you at a place in your life where you hate and grieve over your sin because of the offense it is to God? The Puritan Thomas Watson once said, "We are to find as much bitterness in weeping for sin as we ever found sweetness in committing it"25 Are you willing to take full responsibility for your sin problem and make no excuses? Are you ready to do whatever it takes to put off this sin and put on righteousness? Without a heart of true repentance you will never be able to change. But if you are willing to humble yourself and turn from your sin, you can glorify God with a changed life.

> **May it never be! How shall we who died to sin still live in it? ...Therefore do no let sin reign in your mortal body so that you obey its lusts, and do**

> not go on presenting the members of your body to
> sin as instruments of unrighteousness; but present
> yourselves to God as those alive from the dead,
> and your members as instruments of righteous-
> ness to God. ...Do you not know that when you
> present yourselves to someone as slaves for obedi-
> ence, you are slaves of the one whom you obey,
> either of sin resulting in death, or of obedience
> resulting in righteousness?
> **Romans 6:2, 12-13, 16**

Before temptation hits again:

1. Confess your sins of lust to God and to any others you have sinned against in the process (who are aware of your sin). Explain your willingness to give yourself fully to repentance (putting off your sin and putting on what is right). Then ask for forgiveness (Psalm 51:1-4; Matthew 5:23-24).

2. Daily, even several times a day, ask God to work in this area of your life and help you to put forth full effort toward change (2 Corinthians 9:8).

3. Begin to cultivate a passion for God and regular (daily) worship and Bible meditation/study. Study God's attributes and what Christ has done for you. Learn to walk through your day being mindful of God and His Word (Matthew 22:37).

4. Tell your wife and someone who can be a help to you in your struggle so that you will have accountability. No more secrets (Hebrews 10:24-25).

5. Make a list of helpful verses and truths from this study to meditate on regularly and use when you are tempted (Romans 12:2).

6. Make a list of righteous and loving *thoughts* to put on when lustful thoughts come into your mind. Especially prepare loving thoughts and prayers to apply to those you are tempted to lust after (Ephesians 4:23). For example:
   - "Lord, I pray that this person will come to know you."
   - "Lord, bless this person today. Help them in whatever way is needed."
   - "They are God's creation. I will not use them but serve them. How can I serve this person?"

7. Make a list of ways to show love to your wife (Ephesians 5:25).
8. Make a list of ways to show love to others (Philippians 2:3-4).
9. Make a covenant with God about your eyes (Job 31:1; Psalm 101:3).
10. Take whatever radical steps are needed to make no provision for your flesh (Romans 13:14).
11. Think through the times and situations in which you are normally tempted. Avoid them if at all possible. Prepare for them and get accountability for them if you cannot avoid them (Psalm 119:59-60).
12. Think through your schedule and your normal routine of sin, and think of ways to reorder your life (different places, different activities, a different schedule) as much as possible.
13. Write out a prayer that you can pray when the battle is raging.
14. Write out a prayer that you can pray before times of intimacy with your wife.
15. Find a way to serve in your church (1 Corinthians 12:4-7).
16. Develop other interests and activities that have an element of giving or serving to them. Don't be idle!

At the time of temptation: (F.L.E.E. from sin to God).

1. **F**lee! Act quickly to run away from sin. Acknowledge your complete allegiance to God and put on loving thoughts and actions. Get out of or vary the situation immediately (2 Timothy 2:22).
2. **L**ean on God. Call on Him for strength to honor Him. Draw near to God and He will draw near to you (Psalm 37:5; James 4:8).
3. **E**ntertain the right thoughts (Philippians 4:8-9). Rehearse those things for which you are grateful and thankful.
4. **E**agerly continue to pursue love and righteousness. Don't look back. Look to your "ways to love and serve" lists for ideas if necessary. Engage yourself in giving (Proverbs 21:21).

If you fail and commit sexual sin (in thought or deed):

1. Do not engage in panic, self-pity, or giving up! These attitudes are just what Satan is hoping for, but this is not acceptable to God because it is not in keeping with true repentance, and it will not get you anywhere! Get up and get back on the path to victory if

you are still serious about repentance. You probably will not be flawless in putting off old habits. It takes time to change. It is a serious matter to choose to sin, but all is not lost if you return to a righteous path and refuse to give up (Proverbs 24:16).

2. Ask yourself what God says about your sin and determine how it was *taking* or *using* instead of *giving* and *loving*.

3. Ask yourself, "If I had this to do over again, what would I do?" and "Am I really grieved over my sin because it is against God and because I want to love and serve Him?" Am I really serious about giving full effort to change?

4. Confess your sin to God as abominable before Him, share your desire to repent, and ask forgiveness. Tell Him your plan to keep this from happening again (Psalm 32:5; James 5:16).

5. Thank Christ for already paying the penalty for that sin and for His ability to change you (Romans 7:24-8:1).

**Therefore, having been justified by faith, we have peace with God through our Lord Jesus Christ.
Romans 5:1**

How much do you want to honor Christ with your life? Are you willing to do what God requires? Determination, with dependence on God, is the key. You are assured victory if you *practice* God's principles and depend on His power. Yes, it will be hard work. Is it worth it to you? The hard work required will actually be a good deterrent to turning back to sin. God knows what He is doing by not zapping us out of our sinful habits. The process that you must go through and the discipline you will learn will serve your Christian growth in many ways.

You *can* change. Many have gone before you. As impossible as it may seem now, you must make the commitment to give it everything you've got because you believe God's promises. I can assure you that if you are only partially committed to the task or only willing to do part of what it takes, you will *not* succeed. Repentance is an all or nothing commitment. Give it everything you have, and God will give you His power to cooperate with Him in the change process.

Men, the consequences of this sin are so harmful to your relationship with God and so devastating to your family, that if you do not deal with this sin through repentance, you will regret it. **Do not be deceived.**

> **Therefore we do not lose heart, but though our outer man is decaying, yet our inner man is being renewed day by day. For momentary, light affliction is producing for us an eternal weight of glory far beyond all comparison.**
> **2 Corinthians 4:16-17**

Appendix II

Bi–weekly/Monthly Leadership Worksheet
A Tool for Greater Understanding and Establishing New Habits

When a Christian husband leads his wife and home like Christ he can glorify God, see God work (answers to prayer), and be fulfilled. This worksheet not only lists the areas of leadership that you need to think through, but it also helps you get started by having you chose the regular times for preparation and discussion once or twice a month. With time, one should become more spontaneous - not so structured. Answer the * questions prior to meeting with your wife.

LEADING IN THE MARRIAGE RELATIONSHIP

☐ Set times for preparation and meeting

On what day and at what time will you prepare?

On what day and at what time will you meet with your wife?

Complete the following exercises:

*1. Things I appreciate about her:

*2. Ways I can show sweetheart love to my wife:

*3. My own confessions and personal changes to make:

*4. When I will seek to spend time with her:

5. Things we can do together:

6. My plan to pray with her daily:

7. My plan for intimacy (Next time: transfer what stays the same and add anything new):

   - *A prayer to pray beforehand:

   - * Thoughts to think at the time:

   - Things to say at the time (ask):

   - Ways to prepare her (ask):

   - Ways to please her (ask):

8. Concerns my wife has about the relationship:

*9. Concerns I want to share about the relationship:

10. Spiritual input/direction to share regarding concerns after considering all of it prayerfully:

LEADING MY WIFE
(same preparation time, same meeting time)

☐ Complete the following exercises:

*1. Encouragement to give her:

*2. My own confessions and personal changes to make:

3. Praises from her:

4. Update on delegated areas (finances, children during the day, etc.):

5. When I can spend time in the Word with her regularly:

6. Questions and requests from her:

7. Concerns and prayer requests from her:

8. Ways I can serve her:

9. Tentative plans of hers (freedom whenever possible):

*10. Observations of patterns:

- Are there any observed sin patterns to lovingly and respectfully talk with her about?

- Is more instruction/help/accountability needed?

- If she is a believer, and is not repenting at all, what believer can I bring in that knows and loves her?

- Do I need to bring in a church elder?
  Who?
  When?

*11. Spiritual input and direction to her:

12. Biblical concerns from her about my leadership or life:

PROTECTING AND LEADING OUR HOME
(same preparation time, same meeting time)

☐ Complete the following exercises:

*1. Am I being the greatest servant in my home in attitude and action? How? If not, where, how, and when can I change?

*2. Am I providing food, clothing, shelter, and safety for my family to the best of my ability? Any changes I can pray about and work toward without compromise of Biblical principles?

*3. Is there anything affecting the home adversely (compromises, T.V., schedules, people, reading materials, etc.)?

*4. My own confessions and personal changes to make:

5. Input from wife:

6. Is the home basically and usually operating in order or in chaos? Any specific areas of need?

7. Does my wife believe she is totally equipped to run the home (under my direction)? Is she overwhelmed?

   •   Items needed:

- Training needed:

- Weekly help needed (due to training, physical limitations, home–schooling, multiple births, etc.):

- Ways I can help:

- Accountability needed:

*8. Thoughts or tentative plans to share about decisions/ directions that affect my wife/family:

9. Input from my wife about thoughts or tentative plans/ decisions:

10. Final decisions/directions to share that affect wife/family.
    (If affect whole family will have a family meeting.
    Date:_____)

LEADING MY CHILDREN
Set times for preparation and meeting

On what day and at what time will you prepare?

On what day and at what time will you meet with your children?

☐ Complete the following exercises:

*1. Ways I can show love to him/her:

*2. When I will spend time with him/her:

*3. My own confessions and changes to make:

*4. Encouragement to him/her:

 5. Praises from him/her:

 6. Questions or requests from him/her:

 7. Concerns or prayer requests from him/her:

8. Tentative plans of his/hers (give freedom when possible):

9. Observations of patterns and needs:

    *   Are there any observed sin patterns to lovingly and respectfully talk with him/her about or instruct him/her in?

    *   Is discipline needed? (If so, what?)

    *   Is more instruction/help/accountability needed?

    *   If he/she is a believer, and he/she in not repenting at all, what believer can I bring in who know and loves him/her?

    *   Do I need to bring in a church elder?
        Who?
        When?

10. Direction and spiritual input to him/her:

11. Information or delegation to wife:

12. Biblical concerns from him/her about my leadership or life:

Appendix III

Some Often Used Deceptions Within the Minds of Men

1. The "oops" view = no big deal. It was just a mistake.

2. The "relabeled" view = I wasn't sinfully angry, I was just stressed, or frustrated, or pressured, etc.

3. The "under the bridge" view = what's past is past. We don't need to deal with it now.

4. The various "comparison" views=

    a. Compared with my past - the way I used to be - what's the problem?

    b. Compared with others and their problems - if you think I'm bad, you should look at . . .

    c. Compared to others - they're doing it, so it must be OK for me to do.

    d. Compared with all the good I do - the good far outweighs the bad.

5. The "victim" view = someone or something caused me to sin. I couldn't help it.

6. The "no one's perfect, I'm only human" view = God expects me to act like a fallen human being.

7. The "there's too much in Scripture to obey" view = surely God doesn't really expect me to obey all that is in Scripture.

8. The "it's all taken care of" view = since God paid for all my sins, past, present, and future, I don't have any responsibility to deal with my sin.

9. The "my sin doesn't affect others" view = what's private is private, my sins don't really affect others.

10. The "oh, I may as well sin in my actions" view = since I'm battling sin in my mind and not faring very well, I may as well sin in my actions.

11. The "last time" view = I'm going to go ahead and sin this time, but this will be the last time.

12. The "why are you looking at me?" view = he or she has got the log, so why are you looking at my speck?

13. The "you'd do the same, if you were in my situation" view = I'm unique, my situation is unique, and I just had to sin.

14. The "I confessed it, so why are there consequences?" view = my acknowledging my sin and confessing it ought to remove all consequences.

15. The "I deserve the pleasures that sin offers" view = I'm not getting what I rightfully should have, so I'll sin to get it because I deserve these pleasures.

16. The "sin is not so bad, if no one is around" view = if no one else knows or sees it, it is not that serious.

17. The "God sees my heart and the desire to please Him, so He overlooks my sin" view = when I sin, God sees the good intentions that are there from time to time. If I intend to change or want to change, it's as good as change itself.

18. The "God has changed in His view and treatment of sin" view = God has certainly changed from how He viewed sin in the O.T. and is now much softer and lenient with it for His children.

19. The "I can't obey God unless someone helps me" view = I can't do right unless or until others step in and help.

20. The "kiss and make up" view = God accepts my constant ritual of acknowledging my sin and asking for forgiveness without serious thought as to repentance going on.

21. The "if we're not talking about the sin anymore, then it's not an issue any more" view = it must no longer be an issue if we aren't discussing it. Out of conversation = out of my mind and life.

Appendix IV

Man is Not a Victim

Many men see themselves as little more than a victim of their circumstances. The truth is, *victim* is not a biblical word. Even those who are treated ruthlessly are not referred to as *victims*. There are several aspects of the word *victim* that we need to consider when addressing this view. If a person suffers an unprovoked crime or sin at the hands of someone else, the person suffering *could be* considered a victim in the sense that he is a receiver of unwarranted treatment. Our legal system will certainly designate him the victim of a crime.

But there are wrong ideas usually associated with the word *victim*. Most often, it carries with it the idea of *complete* innocence when referring to the one who has suffered the offense. This is *rarely* the case so far as the *events* are concerned and *never* the case so far as the *heart* is concerned (Psalm 14:2-3). Let me explain by way of an example.

If you are *lawfully* stopped at a traffic light when a drunk driver rear-ends your car, you are certainly legally innocent *in the accident*. The drunk person is obviously breaking the law of God and man by driving while intoxicated and by hitting you. *If*, by the grace of God, you get out of your car and help the drunk person with pure motives until an ambulance comes to examine you both (rather than yelling at him for ruining your bumper), you can still be considered spiritually *innocent in this event*. However, if you become bitterly hateful and consider the drunk to be a worthless person in camparison to you, you are sinning the sin of pride and are, therefore, no longer *innocent in the event*.

I am not saying that God does not respond compassionately when we are wronged. He does (Hebrews 4:14-6; Isaiah 63:9). And, I am not saying that God will not hold the offender fully responsible. He will (Ezekiel 18:2, 20). What I am saying is that we must remember that God sees any reactionary sin on our part during an incident as grievous as well (Romans 12:14-21). And, we must keep an offender's sin in perspective of our own sin against a Holy God.

> But you, why do you judge your brother? Or you
> again, why do you regard your brother with con-
> tempt? For we will all stand before the judgment
> seat of God. For it is written, "as I live, says the
> Lord, every knee shall bow to me and every
> tongue shall give praise to God." So then each
> one of us will give an account of himself to God.
> Therefore let us not judge one another anymore,
> but rather determine this—not to put an obstacle
> or a stumbling block in a brother's way.
> **Romans 14:10-13**

Most people *do* sin in response to another person's sin and most people *do* see their own sin as less offensive than another's. When we have been wronged it can be very helpful to remember that nothing anyone has done to us is worse than our own sin against a holy God. Since any good in our lives can only be accredited to God's work in us (Jeremiah 17:9; Matthew 19:17; 1 Corinthians 4:7), and since our sin was so bad that God allowed His only Son to be killed in order to pay for our sin (2 Corinthians 5:21; 1 Corinthians 15:3), we know that we are *not* in and of ourselves any better than any one else because we sin on a regular basis.

> But now apart from the Law the righteousness of
> God has been manifested, being witnessed by the
> Law and the Prophets, even the righteousness of
> God through faith in Jesus Christ *for all those*
> *who believe; for there is no distinction; for all have*
> *sinned and fall short of the glory of God.*
> **Romans 3:21-23 [emphasis mine]**

Secondly, the word *victim* can imply that a "senseless, never-should-have-happened" event has taken place. The danger here is to forget the loving sovereignty (perfect and purposeful control) of God in one's life. While some events may indeed be tragic, God knows the end from the beginning and how that event can serve to humble a person (Job 42:1-6), draw a person to Himself (John 6:44), show Himself to be a greater-than-anything God (Jeremiah 32:17; Genesis 50:20) and/or reveal Himself to the sufferer as Refuge, Strength and Helper (Isaiah 57:15).

In short, only God has the ability to work all things together for both our good *and* His glory in a fallen world, never ignoring one to achieve the other. We must not take the view that something shouldn't have happened to us. Is God not good? Is God wrong? Is God lacking in power? Obviously none of these are true according to the Bible.

> **And we know that God causes all things to work together for good to those who love God, to those who are called according to His purpose.**
> **Romans 8:28**

Thirdly, the word *victim* often gives a person a hopeless outlook. No one who knows God is without hope, the ability to overcome and the resources to live with joy and thankfulness in spite of what has happened. This must sometimes be taken on faith until the truth and principles of God's Word can be specifically applied to one's situation and thinking (Genesis 50:20; John 20:24-29; 1 Corinthians 10:13; 1 Peter 1:6-7). Unfortunately, some individuals have been taught that they can never lead "normal" lives again. This is tragic because it utterly contradicts Scripture.

> **Grace and peace be multiplied to you in the knowledge of God and of Jesus our Lord; seeing that His divine power *has granted to us everything pertaining to life and godliness*, through the true knowledge of Him who called us by His own glory and excellence. For by these He has granted to us His precious and magnificent promises, *so that by them you may become partakers of the divine nature*, having escaped the corruption that is in the world by lust.**
> **2 Peter 1:2-4 [emphasis mine]**

Finally, the word *victim* usually allows a person to ignore personal responsibility. That brings us back to where we started. To be "a victim of your circumstances" is to declare yourself free from responsibility so far as thoughts, actions, usefulness and life direction are concerned. If we cannot help our responses, we conveniently cannot be held accountable for them. I have heard such statements as, "My sin is actually the result of a 'sickness' that I have because of what happened to me," "I am this way because of my parent's failures," "I turned out this way because we were poor and I was exposed to many bad influences; I didn't have a chance," or " I have a disease or chemical imbalance; that's why I had to sin."

This blame-shifting (whether subtle or not) is a grievous thing to my heart. I listen to these people as they seek to excuse themselves for their sin, knowing that at the same time they are removing all hope for themselves. Very often, people have been encouraged in these wrong beliefs by unbiblical counsel (which can even be "Christian" counsel). The truth is, we *will* be held accountable for our every thought, word, and deed.

> **So then each one of us will give an account of himself to God.**
> **Romans 14:12**

The Bible clearly teaches that we are always responsible for our *own* sin, no matter what our circumstances are—*not* for the sin of others, but for our *own* sin. We cannot say that "so and so" causes us to do what we do. Our own sinful heart simply is given *opportunity* to express itself in our difficult situations. We sin in response to these situations because sin is in us and because we choose to sin. Christians have a double responsibility because through salvation and the application of the Word of God, we don*have* to sin.

> *For he who has died is freed from sin.* **Now if we have died with Christ, we believe that we shall also live with Him, knowing that Christ, having been raised from the dead, is never to die again; death no longer is master over Him. For the death that He died, He died to sin once for all; but the life that He lives, He lives to God. Even so consider yourselves to be** *dead to sin,* **but alive to God in Christ Jesus.**
> **Romans 6:7-11 [emphasis mine]**

Many times the word *victim* allows a person to think of himself wrongly. When a person adopts *the victim mentality*, he usually develops self-pitying, self-righteous, or hopeless attitudes. Those who *know God* and *abide* in His truth *can* lead the kind of life that

God intended, even if they have been greatly wronged. They simply must learn to apply the word of God to their circumstances.

> **And God is able to make all grace abound to you, so that always having all sufficiency in everything, you may have an abundance for every good deed.**
>
> **2 Corinthians 9:8**

Put Off I need to stop...	Put On I need to start...	When I need to practice...	Thoughts I need to renew...	Where Temptation Begins I need to avoid...
Action:	Action:			
Evidences:	Evidences:			
Verses:	Verses:			

FURTHER READING

Masculinity Resources:

Gender Questions, by John Benton. London: Evangelical Press, 2000.

Different By Design, by John MacArthur, Jr. Wheaton, IL: Victor Books, 1994.

Recovering Biblical Manhood and Womanhood, by John Piper and Wayne Grudem. Wheaton, IL: Crossway, 1991.

The Godly Man's Picture, by Thomas Watson. Edinburgh: Banner of Truth, rpt. 1992.

Future Men, by Doug Wilson. Moscow, ID: Canon Press, 2001.

From Boy to Man, by R. Albert Mohler Jr. Louisville, KY: The Southern Baptist Theological Seminary, 2005.

Leadership Resources:

Craftsmen: Skillfully Leading Your Family for Christ, by John Crotts. Wapwallopen, PN: Shepherd Press, 2005.

The Book on Leadership, by John MacArthur. Nashville TN: Thomas Nelson, 2006.

The Exemplary Husband, by Stuart W. Scott. Bemidji, MN: Focus Publishing, 2000.

Equal Yet Different, by Alexander Strauch. Littleton, CO: Lewis and Roth, 1999.

Decision-making Resources:

Decision-making and the Will of God, by Garry Friesen. Portland OR: Multnoma Press, 1980.

Just Do Something, by Kevin DeYoung. Chicago IL: Moody Publishers, 2009.

Is That You Lord? By Garry E. Gilley. Webster, NY: Evangelical Press, 2007

Found: God's Will, by John MacArthur. Wheaton, IL: Victor Books, 1978.

Decision-making God's Way: A New Model for Knowing God's Will, by Garry Meadors. Grand Rapids, MI: Baker Book House, 2003.